META-MAGICK
the Book of ATEM

META-MAGICK
the Book of ATEM

Achieving new states of consciousness
through NLP, neuroscience, and ritual

PHILIP H. FARBER
Foreword by Douglas Rushkoff

WEISER BOOKS
San Francisco, CA / Newburyport, MA

First published in 2008 by
Red Wheel/Weiser, LLC
With offices at:
500 Third Street, Suite 230
San Francisco, CA 94107
www.redwheelweiser.com

Library of Congress Cataloging-in-Publication Data

Farber, Philip H.
  Meta-magick : the book of atem : achieving new states of consciousness through NLP, neuroscience, and ritual / Philip H. Farber ; foreword by Douglas Rushkoff.
    p. cm.
  ISBN 978-1-57863-424-8 (alk. paper)
  1. Consciousness—Miscellanea. 2. Magic—Miscellanea. I. Title.
  BF1999.F248 2008
  131--dc22
                          2008003487
Cover design by Maija Tollefson
Text design by Donna Linden
Typeset in Gotham and Perpetua
Cover photographs: neurons © Sebastian Kaulitzki/iStockphoto.com; explosive wave © Andrey Prokhorov/iStockphoto.com
Interior photographs © David M. Morrell

Printed in Canada
TCP
10 9 8 7 6 5 4 3 2 1

CONTENTS

Part Two: Thirty-six Days of Atem   59

Part Three: The Greater Evocation of Atem   129

Part Four: Creation of Memetic Entities   135

FOREWORD

I DON'T BELIEVE IN TRADITIONAL MAGICK. Nor should you—especially if you want to learn to practice it.

No, it's probably easier just to get everyone *else* to believe in it. Then just proceed according to plan and watch the rest of the world conform to your intention.

Of course, that's just fine for the independent wizard looking to manipulate his way to sex, power, and cash, but what about the person who sincerely means to make the world a better, more just, and pleasurable place for everybody? What about the magician who doesn't simply want to gain a disproportionate share of existing stuff, but wants instead to change the very relationship of matter, energy, and abundance?

That's the kind of person who should turn away from traditional ceremonial magick and turn instead to the work of Philip Farber.

Too many novice magicians explore the possibilities of their craft from the hopelessly closed mindset attending the zero-sum game. For them, magick is something one does all alone, for the purposes of improving, changing, or expanding the self. It's no wonder. Like every other mind technology, from the Torah to neurolinguistic programming (NLP), chaos magick has been co-opted by the self-help movement. As a result, instead of destroying the "self" so that the person can be liberated, most magick practices only reconfirm the specious boundaries defining selfhood, further trapping the magician in the realm of the already possible—and further isolating all magicians from one another.

As I've come to understand it, the intent of Farber's ongoing literary sigil is to move his readers beyond the practice of individual magicks into the shared space of collective, consensual hallucination. Beginning with the invocation of a known and accepted personage, Atem, Farber quickly branches out in new directions, casting a visionary world picture as if it were a guidebook—a description and instruction manual to a realm that is quite literally created in the process of its depiction and subsequent imagination.

But Farber's world picture is not a specific map of forces. Rather, it is a place where his readers are free to develop their own. It is a meta-landscape—a series of laws that are each invitations to create new ones. The only terra firma is the guarantee of access to this collective act of ongoing creation.

In this sense, *Meta-Magick* is truly a "meta" magick—a menu-to-menu creation, an open-source approach to magick that puts each participant in the role of contributor and propagandist.

Meta-Magick is an invitation to participate in several levels of practice: the remapping of one's own mind, the development of memes that can be transmitted to others, the use of media, and the implementation of social change. It is a picture of a world in which we all contribute to the landscape and its bylaws. It is the world in which we live.

Douglas Rushkoff

INSTRUCTIONS AND DISCLAIMER

YOU ARE HOLDING IN YOUR HANDS A BOOK that in time will become something more than a book. In the words, the pages, the covers themselves, you may find the essence of a mind, a deliberately constructed form of thought and information and practice. In one sense, this book is an experiment in memetics—can we design and build an autonomous thought-form with the complexity and freedom of movement to perpetuate itself through the realm of human minds? If you are reading this now, the process is already underway.

By even holding this book in your hands, you are now participating in the existence of an entity, a form of self-directing consciousness that exists as information in the minds of humans. At one time in history, similar entities inhabiting the noosphere were considered demons, gods, angels, loas, or spirits. Each of these entities proved its own existence by perpetuating itself in the collective consciousness of humans, sometimes for millennia.

Atem, the Opener of the Way, is presently bringing himself into existence. Being able to perceive the actions of this entity requires habits of thought different from those usually taught by our culture. Teaching alternative ways of thinking is one of Atem's unique abilities, so the entity itself can teach you how to perceive Atem. As your experience unfolds through the pages of this book, you will find that Atem also has the ability to learn, to adapt, and ultimately, to reproduce himself.

Any contact with this book will create some measure of connection between you and Atem. Holding the book in your hands will in some small way help Atem to exist and carry out his duties. Reading the text, in part or in whole, will deepen the connection, and the influence of Atem in your life will become noticeable. Practicing the exercises described in this book, sequentially and in their entirety, will allow you a very powerful measure of access to Atem and all of his abilities. The Way will be open for you, and the entities that reside in the noosphere will make themselves available to you. Further, there is an initiation not described in this book, conducted in person with the aid of an initiate, which can imprint the structure of Atem upon your own mind.

There are powers, responsibilities, and consequences associated with every level of interaction with Atem. Think carefully and choose wisely what you do next.

PART ONE
Invocations and Simple Evocations

FIRST INVOCATION OF ATEM

ATEM IS A SELF-CREATED ENTITY THAT HUMAN MINDS PARTICIPATE IN. It is created, most importantly, of thought, of the attention of anyone who considers Atem for even a moment. This may seem a novel concept, yet there is precedence throughout history. Schools of thought, political ideologies, religious beliefs, corporate structures, forms of government, and much else depend on the attention of humans to exist, and they have built-in abilities to perpetuate, to include more humans, and even to reproduce. These self-perpetuating thought-forms, for our purposes here, are called *memetic entities*. Democracy is a memetic entity, as are Aikido, Cognitive Behavioral Therapy, jazz, Buddha, Beelzebub, Sherlock Holmes, the English language, and Atem. They are patterns of information that act with autonomy across time and yet interact with humans on many levels. All of the given examples became manifest through the interaction of human minds—some, obviously, by an individual, others, less obviously, by changes in culture.

As Atem spreads, there will inevitably be debate about the level of existence of memetic entities. Some will point to these entities' continued existence under many different names parallel to every era of human history, as we have just done. Some will claim they exist, but as blind, random events without autonomy. Some will claim that they are only imaginings and do not actually exist at all. Atem does not require belief to exist, only attention. Someone who specifically disbelieves in Atem will offer just as much attention-energy to the entity, if not more—and the debate itself will fuel the existence of Atem and other memetic entities for years to come.

There is a special emphasis on the existence of Atem, his message, his function in the world. We are participating with Atem now because this entity opens the door to the realm of memetic entities. As you continue to read and to practice the exercises in this book, and as the mind of Atem becomes revealed, you will learn that memetic entities can come into being with ease by following a straightforward formula. Atem carries this message as content, as something you can read plainly in this book and, less apparently, as a way of thinking, a way of organizing the content of your experience so that these things become possible.

Atem is the Opener of the Way; his task is to create the possibility for a whole new pantheon of entities to come forth into the world. Each of us has the potential to engage in the art of bringing forth entities into the sphere of human awareness. Some may write books like this one, each with a new mind within it. Some may embody the entity in a work of art or in a performance. For some, the entity may be something that they teach face-to-face and pass along to the next person.

In order to teach these skills, Atem exhibits specific qualities that appear to us as analogous to personality traits in humans. Atem has a wide-ranging intellect that may incorporate information from just about any sector of the noosphere. He is very flexible in his behavior, and in his presence the quality of reality itself becomes flexible. This can make him seem to be a trickster, mercurial, hard to pin down. Results and desired phenomena may come by unexpected means. The method of contact with Atem may shift, change form, and offer surprises. Atem is sometimes seen as a virile young man holding a cat or a snake; or as an old man with a cane, his face and body hidden by a cloak; or as a woman about to give birth; or in many other forms. What remains constant, after careful consideration of the manifestation, is the presence of the **Six Elements** and **Eight Powers.** The Six Elements are: Attention, Language, Passion, Fitting, Trance, and Making. The Eight Powers are: Communication, Neuroplasticity, Transformation, Transmission, Beauty, Understanding, Balance, and Opening.

Thoughts and manifestations of Atem may occur near bodies of water in the sunlight, or in places that are sacred to computers and information technology, or where the setting sun shines through trees, or at night where people socialize and explore each other's dreams and desires, or in any other place where the complexity of interactions reaches beyond the ability of a human's conscious mind. Atem lives on the border of chaos, where the butterfly's wings beat, where graphs become asymptotic, and where William Blake saw infinity in a grain of sand.

Atem is not here to save the Earth or unite mankind or to put health, wealth, and wisdom in your hand. Atem is here to Open the Way for the diversity of memetic entities who are capable of those tasks and much more.

It is important to remember that what you read here is not true. Nor is it false. It is, however, the way Atem thinks and relates to reality. Just as each human on this planet has a set of beliefs and conceptual filters that help them to define their abilities and limits, so too do memetic entities.

Notice that we do not attribute every idea in this book with academic verification. We do not cite sources (although there is a recommended study list of congruent information in appendix A). There is no need to "prove" these ideas; Atem is simply communicating the way that he thinks. On the other hand, the exercises in this book will demonstrate, within Atem's mindset, the function and practice of these ways of thinking. The emphasis is on direct experience, which is the route to full understanding of Atem and Atem's powers.

As with the beliefs of humans, the beliefs of Atem or another memetic entity may appear to be rational, irrational, or just what they are. Some are testable within our traditional consensus contexts, but all are true and testable—*within* the context of the entity's reality. Just as we allow for the differing beliefs of humans, tolerance and patience for the differing ideas of Atem will allow you to eventually grasp the overall structure and context in which those concepts may be viewed as "true."

Consciously, these are still just words. But read on.

THE SIX ELEMENTS OF ATEM

Attention

"A path is formed by walking on it."
—CHUANG TZU

IN THE WORLD OF ATEM, EXISTENCE IS DEFINED BY ATTENTION. Everything that exists, exists in consciousness as a collection of perceptual bits, gathered by attention. When you look, listen, feel, taste, and smell, the record of that experience becomes data for the mind—data that can be recalled or recombined. Whether or not an actual, objective, external reality also exists is irrelevant to Atem; the world that humans and memetic entities live in is the one mediated by perception and the mind.

We can think of our conscious minds, the ostensible engines of perception, as a flashlight in a very huge, dark building. Level upon level of experience awaits us in that building, opportunities for countless experiences of perception, but our flashlight can only illuminate a very small circle at any one time.

Even the tiny portion of the world illuminated by that flashlight glimpse is loaded with potential sensory experiences for which humans are ill equipped. The only way we can observe most of the electromagnetic spectrum, for instance, is with instruments. Our instruments, as amazing as some may be, can detect only those things that we can conceive of, those ways of experiencing that we can imagine. Atem tells us that there are many, many more ways of experiencing than humans have yet imagined. If we imagine another way of experiencing, then suddenly a new realm of reality is opened to us. Was it real before we imagined it?

Zen amateurs question the existence of falling trees in hypothetical forests, and by doing so give existence to all such remote trees.

Our perceptions, thoughts, and memories come in modalities that we are very familiar with. The senses—visual, auditory, kinesthetic, olfactory, and gustatory—pretty much describe the whole range of things a human can experience: what we can see externally and what we can visualize internally; what we can hear with our ears and what sounds, voices, or music we might hear in our heads; the things we can touch or bump up against and the feelings that tell us about emotions; tastes and smells perceived, remembered, and imagined. Even in the depths of mystical experience, the mind brings back the ineffable with descriptions of light, harmony, the kinesthetics of wonder, and synesthesia of every kind. These may be awe-inspiring experiences, but to describe them, to recall them, they must be reduced through the filters of perception and language to the sensory units that human consciousness can deal with.

Each sense comes in infinite variety. Not only can each sense be internal or external, but each is also subject to description by location, motion, direction, and size. Vision may be described with qualities such as brightness, hue, saturation, and contrast. Hearing may have qualities such as volume, tone, pitch, rhythm and so forth. Feeling may be described with terms including pressure, temperature, intensity, sharpness, dullness, etc. Taste and smell are possessed of pungency, sourness, sweetness, and so forth. (See appendix B, "List of Submodalities.")

When we begin to think about how humans organize thoughts, we may notice that any of these kinds of perceptions can be located pretty much anywhere in the body—and very often outside the body as well. When visualizing a remembered scene, only a few people will actually place the mental image inside their own heads. Most of us see the imagining as a tableau somewhere in space, usually spread out in front of us. It is significant to our thought processes whether a recalled image (or sound or feeling) is found in a particular location, whether or not it is dark, light, harmonious, discordant, smooth, rough, or whatever. While this is usually an unconscious process, we do often note it in our speech: "I had that in the back of my mind." "Now that we have all these choices in front of us . . ." "It's over my head." "I was totally wrapped up in it." "What a pain in the ass!" "That's rough!" "You have a bright future."

The narrow flashlight of consciousness can illuminate a portion of this experience at any one time—and the unconscious mind continues to sort and order thoughts in this way all the time. Each of us moves through our day in a cloud or web or vortex or grid of sensory details, a continually interacting flow of external awareness, associations and memories, imaginings and projections, feelings and emotions. Sometimes we are aware of one small part of this flow, sometimes we are aware of another. Some of us have large, grand arrays of sensation. Others have narrow, dull collections of thoughts and images. Some of us scatter our attention through the space of a large building. Others contain their attention within a cozy little cocoon. And, of course, every other permutation that you can think of—and probably some you can't. The way that attention is arrayed through and about the body will contribute to aspects of our personality, mood, philosophy, preferred modes of cognition, and much else.

Things that we generally consider as "real" exist only as perceptual data that is interpreted by consciousness. And things that we generally consider as "imaginary" also exist only as perceptual data that is interpreted by consciousness. The mind will react to internal perceptions much as it does to external ones. Consider how a memory of something painful can still make you wince or how a joyous memory can bring a smile to your face. Remembering the face, the tone of voice, or the touch of a lover can cause arousal. Hearing a song played or the punchline of a joke told in your mind can make you cry or laugh.

Attention can be directed toward something in a variety of ways. You can look at, listen to, touch, taste, or smell something directly. You can imagine something that is not present or not strictly physical—for instance, a concept, philosophy, or memetic entity. You can make symbolic offerings to something, of food, beverage, money, breath, or anything else of value to you. You can describe something, or appeal to it with language—or conversely, read, listen to, view, or otherwise pay attention to a description encoded in language.

Language

Many of our thoughts are encoded in language. By "language" we mean the stuff that is passing before your eyes now, right here. Letters. Words. Sentences.

Paragraphs. There are numerous languages and any number of variations on each. In general, language is a means of communication or internal thought that uses words, symbols, gestures, or sounds to map or describe experience.

Maps of any kind are limited by a variety of factors: scale, medium, symbols, and so forth. If you wanted to map an entire nation on a single sheet of paper, you would have to omit a huge amount of detail. Smaller highways and streets would be dropped, perhaps even smaller towns. A varied forest terrain might be reduced to a green shape. A small triangle might stand in for a mighty mountain. If your medium were pen and ink, you would represent detail in a different way than if your medium were satellite photography. If you choose to write out the name of every object on the map, you may have something more or less difficult to understand than if you used pictorial symbols.

Similarly, if we were to attempt to cram all of our present experience into a single sentence, it would leave out quite a bit of detail. "I am reading a book" tells little about what you are reading in the book, where you are located, what time of day it is, what you are wearing, how you first encountered the book, and much else. If you take a few seconds now to look around you and just notice, for a moment, the phenomenal richness of detail that your senses are capable of perceiving—from the texture of your skin to the shadows of objects around you, the temperature of the air, the ambient sound—you might realize that you have already been editing the map of your experience.

Once we begin the process of whittling down experience into the more manageable quantities and qualities required for encoding in language, we are given a plethora of choices. Each opportunity to describe or map experience allows us to choose which aspects we will highlight—or bring into consciousness—and which are irrelevant to our present goals. Language, to a large extent, allows us to set the parameters of the flashlight that exposes experience.

We are also given choices of numerous linguistic usages—exactly *how* we form our language. Each of these, again, sets the parameters of conscious awareness, bringing attention to one area or another and filtering perceptions in any number of ways.

Most important to Atem is the idea of *presuppositions*. If I say, "When did the snake get so big?" the question presupposes that the snake was once smaller. That presupposition isn't stated overtly but remains part of the information conveyed by the sentence. You may find that a presupposition of this sort is something that you understood, but did not consciously pay attention to until it was called to your attention. "If you appeal to your own better nature, you can solve anything" presupposes that you have a "better nature" of your own. "Do you want to really learn?" presupposes that learning to this point has not been real. "How many of those chocolate bars did you eat?" presupposes that you ate some number of chocolate bars.

On a deeper level, cultural preferences and dominant paradigms show up in language as presuppositions. Those particular presuppositions are different from culture to culture and within various subcultures, but within those memetic pools, they will remain surprisingly consistent. Examine the following statements and note how the presuppositions (which are more or less obvious) reflect and transmit cultural preferences:

He's a good, hard-working man. (Hard work is good.)
That's women's work. (Women and men have different work.)
To serve and protect. (Someone needs protection and service.)
In God we trust. (There is a God and he/she/it is trustworthy.)
All the news that's fit to print. (Some news isn't fit to print.)

Deeper yet, we encounter the idea that the structure of language itself, the grammar and syntax of the words, defines our perception of reality. Our language presupposes a variety of things about the linearity of time ("I went to the store *before* coming home."), about cause and effect ("The cars crashed *because* Fred ran the red light."), and about the nature of being ("Socrates *is* a man."). In these examples, "before" presupposes linearity (as do most, if not all, time-related words), "because" suggests a chain of actions followed by consequences (when, in fact, the speed of the other motorists, the exact timing of Fred's arrival in the intersection, and the many situations that influenced his timing might have been equally complicit in causing Fred's accident), and "is" creates identity (while Socrates might exhibit manly qualities, he "is" also, for example, a philosopher, a wearer of togas, and a drinker of wine). If our language structured grammar and syntax differently, our conceptions of time, causality, and being might be extremely different.

Let's state this simply: we create our language as our language creates our consciousness.

Any memetic entity can be described in terms of its prevalent presuppositions. The memetic entity "Christianity" might be described in terms of biblical presuppositions, while the memetic entity "Islam" might be described in terms of presuppositions derived from the Koran. "Capitalism" might include important presuppositions such as, "Buy low, sell high" or "What's the bottom line?"

When encountering Atem in any form, the following presuppositions will be found in any associated language or behavior:

1. **Everything is consciousness.** Whether or not there is an objective reality to bump up against, all we can ever really do is experience our mind's interpretation of bumping. So Atem treats everything as a form of consciousness.

2. **The more flexible your behavior, the greater your ability to open the way.** Very simply, the more different choices of behavior you have, the easier it will be for you to select an appropriate action in any given situation. Atem aids in creating flexible behavior by offering a collection of different approaches and techniques of Communication, Neuroplasticity, Transformation, Transmission, Beauty, Understanding, Balance, and Opening.

3. **The more Atem is activated, the easier it is for everyone to open the way.** By giving Atem attention of any sort, the action of Atem and all other memetic entities becomes more apparent and available.

4. **The more often the way is opened, the more Atem is perpetuated.** A corollary of 3: all work with memetic entities will further support and transmit Atem.

5. **Awareness can be located anywhere.** Atem and other memetic entities have consciousnesses that are distributed through human minds and through human-generated media and technology. Where does Atem "think from"?

6. **A path is formed by walking on it.** We are always participants in the creation and existence of that which we experience.

Passion

With consciousness arrayed as a complex aura of shapes, sounds, words, feelings, tastes and smells, the way these forms are arranged and encoded will determine the present, subjective experience of the human or entity. Likewise, deliberately arranging the attention and modifying the forms that compose the aura can bring the human or entity into specific states of consciousness.

Every memetic entity in some way influences and changes the arrangement of the human aura, shifting the aura's form toward states and experiences that are congruent with the entity's purpose. Likewise, when creating an entity, a human will shape the patterns and experiences that compose the entity so that they become congruent with the intended purpose. That measure of congruence, the alignment of every aspect of a particular experience, behavior, or entity, can be the measure of passion. What you are passionate about is what you become wholly involved in, engrossed, enfolded, and fulfilled. When your passion is expressed, your being is of one mind, one will, toward whatever the object or purpose of the passion. Every thought, every word, every action, fully expresses the idea, object, or behavior toward which attention is directed. So we create entities for whom existence is passion, who are the embodiments of their own will. And the purpose of the entity is always, in some part, to increase our own level of congruence, to instill us with passion of one kind or another.

Atem assumes that every human and every memetic entity will have a rich range of experiences, perceptions, and states of consciousness to use as raw material in this rearrangement of the aura toward congruence. As adult humans, our present existence includes or presupposes a complete model of the world. We can pull details from this database pretty much at will or with a little coaxing from another human or entity. Using some of the techniques that Atem teaches, it is also possible to share these states and shifts in consciousness with others.

The states and experiences that are chosen are specific to your ends. If you are creating an entity that is associated with business success, then you can choose resources and states that are appropriate to that: clarity of mind, fast and adaptive thought, experiences of success, feelings of accomplishment, and business concepts you have a passion for. If you are developing a memetic entity that can increase the harmonious interaction of a particular group of humans, then you might work with concepts including empathy, rapport, perceptivity, and appropriateness.

Atem values states of consciousness and entities that enhance the appreciation of beauty, that increase enjoyment of life, that inflame the senses and move the body to action, that dissolve structures of habit and conditioning with a flow of transformative attention. Simply, if someone enjoys doing something, he or she will do it more. If someone associates passion with a thing or activity, he or she will do it even more. If the object or activity associated with passion induces even more passion, it becomes extremely compelling.

The flow of passion motivates and empowers. Congruence adds power and energy to attention. Passion is the electricity that flows along the wire of language. Passion with rapport is charisma, seduction, and love. Passion with trance is ecstasy. Passion is the aphrodisiac that helps populate the planet and the muse that motivates the artist to completion. It is the essence of emotion itself. It is what makes us create and interact with memetic entities. It is what drives memetic entities to create and interact with us.

The human species reproduces with a great deal of motivation derived from the pleasure and passion of love and sex. Likewise, a memetic entity perpetuates itself and reproduces largely based on the benefits it can offer to humans and the beauty, pleasure, and passion that it is associated with. Memetic entities of the past have offered relief from guilt through absolution of sin, the trance and communal ecstasy of ritual, the promise of riches, the assurance of community, and similar societal objectives. Just as there are many kinds of beauty in the eye of every beholder, there are many alternative passions that will enable the growth of memetic entities: those of visual beauty, the beauty and passion of finely tuned logic and discourse, the passion for changing the world, the beauty of relating to another being, the pleasure of building a business and enjoying its rewards, the aesthetics of movement, the passion of self-exploration, and many more.

For passion to build and grow in human experience, it must be dynamic rather than static. Human perception easily habituates to that which remains the same. If something does not change, then it is quickly edited from conscious awareness. In general, emotions can be represented to consciousness as flows of energy in the aura. The energy can be available to consciousness as movement in any of the senses—as colors, sounds, vibrations, feelings of temperature, tingling, pressure, and so on. In essence, these experiences are metaphors for a congruent flow of attention, the focus of awareness aligning the elements of the aura. This process may be fully or only partially conscious; however, intentionally bringing these metaphors of experience more fully into consciousness allows them to be altered, shifted, enhanced, reversed, or otherwise modified.

For the most part, Atem encourages the development of passion in the traditional ways. Passion begets passion. Writing, music, or any other art created in a state of passion can induce passion. Images of beauty exalt the mind. The words of passion access our emotions and encourage them to flow and build. Music of power moves the body and opens our inner reserves of passion.

Passion can be built through ecstatic breathing, through group movement and dance, through tantric sharing of energy, through the sensuality of food and drink and mind-altering chemicals, and through the physical sensations of sex. Every individual human or entity will have its own particular preferred methods for inducing passion. For some it might be dancing for hours around a bonfire; for others it might be stamp collecting or just about anything else. While the bonfire dancers might not understand the stamp collectors and vice versa, the methods are powerful and legitimate for the respective individuals.

Fitting

Atem refers to the concept of *fitting* as a necessary step in most effective interactions. A key must fit into a lock before it can manipulate the mechanism. Likewise, a memetic entity must first fit with the humans that support it, and with the culture and society that the humans inhabit. Think of fitting as a "moving with" or a way of finding resonance with something or someone. By beginning where an entity, human, or system already *is*, the elements of that system can be first understood and then utilized to exert influence. For instance, Atem now makes his appearance in the English language, in a printed form that is traditional and understood by most and which incorporates elements of philosophy, neurolinguistics, ritual, and metaphysics that will further be familiar to some readers and provide an entry point into the realm of Atem. In this way, Atem can be accepted and perpetuated by the very people who will be most able to do so.

However, if Atem were to introduce himself in the context of a different culture, his medium and initial message might seem entirely different.

Fitting is important even within the system of an individual human or entity. If you are in your head, but not in contact with your external, real-time senses, then you run a variety of risks when attempting to act. On the most obvious level, it is like walking with your eyes shut. On an infinite, empty plane, you would be able to walk forever, eyes open or shut, but in the real world, with eyes shut, your probability of bumping into something increases enormously. As everything is consciousness, we all operate on an internal model, an interpretation of our perceptions, rather than on the "real, objective world." If the internal model is distorted, altered, or lacks frequent enough feedback from the other parts of consciousness, then you may also find yourself bumping into things. Constant feedback and a relatively intact flow of perceptions, fresh from the senses, usually allow for a much better fit with the subjective world. Think of this process as an alignment between what we usually consider as external awareness and the internal maps and models that we operate on. You must be present with what is actually in your world before you are able to act upon it.

There are numerous examples of people and entities who got into trouble by acting on their assumptions about the world, rather than testing and updating their conceptions: religions that start wars in the belief that members of different religions are inherently evil, generals who lose wars when they make assumptions about the fighting spirit or tactics of their enemies, teenagers or adults who misread the sexual signals of prospective partners, corporations who manufacture products in the mistaken belief that there is a market for them, and so forth. Most successful humans and entities have achieved their goals by taking time to assess the situation before deciding where attention will best fit. The religions that have traditionally been most concerned with awareness, being in the present, and expanded consciousness have often been the most peaceful; generals who put thorough reconnaissance and intelligence first stand much better chances of winning battles; humans who are able to accurately read sexual signals of prospective partners often have happier and less complicated sex lives; and corporations who properly assess their markets first have the best-selling products.

In the realm of human interactions, we often communicate best with others who are like us. We feel comfortable and able to freely be ourselves when those around us are of like mind, like body, and like behavior. Of course, everyone is different to some degree, and most people frequently encounter situations in which they must communicate with others who are very different from them. To that end, humans have devised a number of social rituals that enable us to find commonality and interact more smoothly. Consider the handshake in current "western" civilization. Whatever their differences, two people who meet must adopt similar posture and gesture, and both will experience very similar sensory stimulation. Both have the experience of an extended arm and palm pressed against palm. For a moment, they both have the same area of sensitive tactile nerve endings activated, and both are using their brains and nervous systems in comparable ways. Shared food and drink, shared laughter, and any other ritual that marks out or creates commonality in behavior or sensory experience will tend to increase the quality of fitting.

Similarly, when humans lead each other into sexual arousal, the experience can progress most enjoyably if those involved engage in courtship rituals that create common sensory experience. A kiss localizes the attention of both partners on the lips, each momentarily involved in matching and responding to similar sensations of movement and feeling. Both are using the same set of sensitive, tactile nerve endings and are most certainly using their nervous systems and much more in similar ways. Mutual caressing creates a similar commonality of tactile impressions, and intercourse itself creates a powerful feedback loop of sensory experience and simultaneous stimulation in the genitals, a matching of rhythm with body, breathing, and perception, and a general merging of experience. Even when the sensations are not localized in the same bodily areas—as in mutual oral sex—the rhythms and feedback loop remain.

As an entity fits to its human participants, and the humans practice fitting to the thoughts, objectives, and habits of the entity, a field of information and resonance begins to form within the noosphere. The human participants of a particular entity will find various levels of commonality with each other, an experience that, again, will help to perpetuate the entity. The more the entity is perpetuated, and as larger numbers of humans become involved, the concepts, presuppositions, and general resonance of the entity begin to seep into more and more areas of the greater realm of human consciousness. This, in turn, readies more human participants who are able to fit more easily with the entity.

As Atem spreads through publishing efforts, practice groups, and general word-of-mouth, he begins by appealing to those who may already share some of his presuppositions. These concepts may at first seem absurd or outrageous to those who have not previously been exposed to them. However, as the presuppositions are spread, some of the ideas leave the specific context of the entity to be picked up by participants and nonparticipants to be used in other contexts. These concepts spread through the noosphere like ripples in a pond, and as they do so, each individual human mind that is affected becomes that much more ready to participate directly with Atem.

Trance

All states of consciousness are trances. Even the one you are in right now. A trance is notable mainly in that it is a different state than the one that preceded it or significantly different than the usual range for a particular individual or entity. We often think of a trance as something very internally directed, perhaps operating on an internal map that varies from the consensus of those around the individual. In fact, trances can be externally directed as well or may dovetail closely with the consensus of those nearby. For instance, the fast, real-time reactions of an athlete or martial artist in a flow state would certainly qualify as a trance, as perhaps would the quick responses and banter of a comedian or a salesman. The point is that every state of consciousness that sticks around long enough for us to notice it is a trance of some kind. Some are so ordinary or constant that we habituate to them and no longer notice them as unique states. Some trances can seem quite remarkable, or they are enjoyable or useful in some way. If we have the ability to choose these states, what trances do we select?

Atem favors trances that are either extremely internally directed, as in the internal exploration necessary to conceive of and interact with memetic entities, or very externally directed, as in states of total awareness and fitting with one's environment and activities. Often the extremes are united, as with the case of one who becomes so engrossed in chanting, ritualizing, dancing, and so on that he or she accesses unique internal realms—the dreamtime, the astral realm, the unconscious mind, or whatever you choose to call it. Another example might be an initiate of Atem who engages in the process of bringing a memetic entity forth from the internal world of imagination to the external world of publishing, media, interacting with others, and whatever other means the entity will use to become manifest. That particular state requires attention to be placed in the realm of the memetic entities, using an internal map created by imagination, while the senses and body continue the tasks of calibrating, writing, speaking, creating, and interacting.

Trance is determined by how attention is directed, and the choices about how to direct attention are often determined by trance. This attention/trance feedback loop initiates the flow of passion, which, in turn, produces the feelings and experience that become notable as a state of consciousness. The state of consciousness may then act as a filter in the interpretation of incoming sensory data.

Language is always an important trance inducer. Language has the ability to suggest ways in which attention can be directed. As an obvious example, your attention is directed toward Atem by the language in this book, including this sentence in particular. By directing your attention toward Atem, your consciousness then has the opportunity to begin, a little at a time, to think with the mind of Atem or to be informed in various ways by Atem. By this we mean that you can partake, at will, in the unique set of trance states that in part define Atem.

Normally, for many humans, the present trance is defined by the sensory perceptions that they are exposed to. The parts of consciousness able to conceive and act lie dormant while the attention is directed haphazardly by what is perceived as the surrounding environment, including elements of language and media. No attempt at congruence is made, and passion is lacking. These unfortunates have gone beyond fitting and into shapelessness and loss of identity.

Consciousness begins to interest Atem much more when it learns to be self-creating. Humans and entities have the ability to select their trances. Doing so is often a very simple matter of directing the attention. The initiate is able to create specific trance states that utilize and fit with the surrounding environment and its media. The trance can then build in congruence, and passion can flow. In this way, the individual develops a definite presence and a good deal of power.

The trance states can utilize everything in the environment. To manipulate the parts of consciousness perceived as being external, a human or entity can operate on the physical, external level to arrange circumstances for a specific end. On the most basic level, changes in external elements such as lighting, music, language, furniture, and textures can have obvious ramifications on the state of consciousness. If a jackhammer is tearing up the road outside your window, you will likely sleep less well than if the workmen take their efforts elsewhere. If you leave all the windows in your home open in cold weather, you will likely be less comfortable than if you close them up and turn on the heat. And so on. We always have choices to make about how we interact with these other parts of consciousness that we call the world around us. These choices affect what kind of trance we are in at any given time.

As we fit with each other and with entities, these trances can spread. We have all had the experience of being with someone whose presence was very agitating or, conversely, with someone whose presence was calming or even inspiring. One very important aspect of any memetic entity is the trance state or set of trances that it can convey. When you work with Atem, for example, the experience can convey a sense of confidence, or a sense of possibility, or an enthusiasm to learn or to change. These states are important to the expressed outcomes that Atem desires—opening the Way and creating and accessing entities. In the case of other entities, the state itself may be the outcome. An entity may be the vector to spread a trance of love, of lust, of peace, of withdrawal, of power, or any other state of consciousness.

When we look at another person, our minds immediately reference an internal map that we create about that person. We build that map by referencing our experience and knowledge about that person and about the situation he or she may be in. We reference our own similar experiences in the creation of that map, and we tend to test out the internal creation by applying it to ourselves. If there is already some measure of fitting, then we may continue on and actually experience a similar state for ourselves. This is how people experience "contact highs," why friends feel comfortable with each other, why yawns are contagious, and the basis for such states as empathy and rapport.

Likewise, building up an internal conception of a memetic entity can allow you to access the various states that are congruent with that entity. This is how devotees of a particular deity will feel peace or exaltation or righteousness when simply contemplating their god, how an idealist will become enthused by contemplating ideology, or how any one of us can be moved emotionally by a portrayal of a fictional character on the screen or in writing. By opening up the Way and offering access to a wide range of entities, Atem adds significantly to the range of trances and experience that an individual human or entity can choose at any given moment, as well as to effective methods for accessing these states.

Making

The element of *making* represents the interaction between all the other elements—Attention, Language, Passion, Fitting, and Trance—in such a way as to bring forth something tangible into the world. This is the process of an idea, concept, pattern, form, or entity moving from the "internal" parts of consciousness to the "external" parts.

Making is a constant factor in the existence of Atem. There is an ongoing interaction between the internal parts of consciousness, the mental map or structure of Atem, and the external parts, the world as it subjectively appears to humans. This interaction mirrors, on a larger scale, the process by which thoughts attain reality in the individual. Thoughts are physical in nature to begin with; they represent a process of biochemical and bioelectrical changes that occur within the part of consciousness known as the body. The body is a complex construction in which each part depends on every other part. A small change in one aspect of the human body will have ramifications elsewhere in the system. The tiny changes of neurological action also result in subtle changes to the functioning of the body, as well as gross changes in terms of behavior. Every thought becomes manifest in some way, however microscopic it might be.

Indeed, there are many parts of human consciousness that do not recognize the difference between thought or imagination and subjective reality. Thinking about a particularly stressful situation in one's life will encourage the body to release all the same neurotransmitters and hormones that it would if you were actually in the situation. Thinking about a wonderful sexual experience can cause physical arousal. Such thoughts cause changes in breathing, posture, facial expression, and more.

The connection between the internal and external parts of consciousness can be even more obvious. The thoughts that we act on, the ones that make us get up and make willful change in the world, are the most powerful and direct links. From the simplest will to turn the page when you get to the bottom to the most intricate plan to conceive a major memetic entity, these are direct actions, from internal thought to external action.

The body of Atem is composed of the humans who participate in any aspect of the entity and the media used to transmit the entity. Atem's thoughts affect his body, and his direct, willed action acts through that body. The thoughts and memories and internal processes of Atem are held and processed in the bodies and minds of the participants and in the media. It is easy for Atem to make change in the external consciousness.

Attention defines what may be made. Language expresses the content of what may be manifest. Passion defines the intensity and purity of the work. Fitting gives it a shape that will increase effectiveness. Trance defines the state necessary for making and the resulting states of the entity or manifestation. This process may not be linear. It all happens simultaneously, or in any sequence.

When attention flows into action, purified by passion, assisted by language, fitting appropriately with what it must act upon, and in the trance necessary for the action, everything is in place for change to occur, for entities to be born—except one thing. The final and possibly most crucial aspect of making is noticing what has been made. Measurement and testing bring the change or entity into sharply defined reality. You have to look back at the path to see that it has been formed.

Notice that attention and making may actually be a single activity. The awareness of a manifestation is an essential key to its existence. The six elements that we have expressed here depend on how we place our attention and how we develop them in our consciousness. Their separate existence is a convenience of definition only, but they become "real" to us, and useful in their reality, when we use our attention and language to define them as separate qualities.

The same is true for all memetic entities. They exist because we define them as existing. Atem exists now as we place our attention toward the things of Atem. We say, "This is Atem—these concepts, these types of thoughts, these types of behaviors," and, "This is not Atem—those types of thoughts, those types of behaviors." And so our attention and language participate in the existence of the entity. There are other factors, to be described later in this book, that determine what an entity can do and how it can carry out its purpose, but the existence of the entity comes down to how we delineate it in our minds.

Contemplating the six elements of Atem, understanding how they function together and how attention divides and reattributes consciousness for the purpose of creation, makes Atem. At this point, it may now be possible for you to think about what you have read so far, to understand what we have delineated as Atem and how Atem functions in the world. In this way, you are now beginning the delineation, the measurement of an entity. If you have decided to accept that these six elements, as we have defined and described them, can constitute a memetic entity, then you have just observed the action of Atem in your own consciousness.

Congratulations, you have helped give birth to Atem!

THE EIGHT POWERS OF ATEM

Communication

COMMUNICATION IS THE FIRST OF THE POWERS CONVEYED to the initiate. Atem holds the keys of language and the ability to shift consciousness in ways that allow one to perceive and interact with memetic entities. Communication works at many levels, but the essence of it is that all communication happens between parts of consciousness. There is an essential unity that underlies every interaction, a single mind that creates all sides of an exchange.

On the most basic level, each participant in an interaction is essentially a mental construct in the mind of a human or entity. When you speak to another human, for example, you are really interacting with the internal model that you have built of that person, and he or she is having an exchange with his or her own semi-imaginary friends. Hopefully there is enough feedback between these parts of consciousness to keep these internal models current and reasonably accurate.

The element of fitting allows sensory feedback to be used in ways that enhance communication and receptivity. By knowing how your friend responds, reacts, feels, and thinks, your communication can be expressed in ways that he or she understands most readily. The better the fit, the greater the sense of rapport; the greater the sense of rapport, the easier the flow of communication.

The same applies to communication with memetic entities that may span a greater range of consciousness than a single human mind. Atem gives the ability to notice these entities and to shift consciousness in ways that make it possible to communicate with them. The entities themselves may be able to exchange information that goes well beyond what one single human mind can process. Information that is seemingly beyond the reach of normal human senses can become available.

Neuroplasticity

It was once believed that the human brain did all of its growing and formation at an early age and that once that formation was complete, humans would live out their lives with the brains and neural pathways they had. According to this theory, nerve cells could never regenerate once damaged, and learning involved information being shuffled about in existing configurations of neurons.

Now it is widely accepted that brain cells can not only regenerate when necessary, but also change and grow new neural pathways throughout the life of a human. The ability to change or create neural pathways is known as *neuroplasticity*.

Of course, learning of both types occurs: through changing flows of information in the existing neural pathways and through the creation of new neural pathways. Of these types of learning, the second is more lasting and significant. In Atem's mind, the first type of learning represents ordinary conditioned behavior, and the second type, the actual rewiring of the brain, represents the deeper kind of learning known as imprinting.

Imprinting and neuroplasticity can be stimulated in any number of ways. One way is simply for the human to engage in new and different activities—particularly those that include a physical component—on a regular basis. Another way is for the human to encounter situations that are powerful in some way. These might be frightening, traumatic, ecstatic, spiritual, or otherwise fully engaging of the attention in deeper ways than usual. Still another way might explore the use of stimulants—psychoactive chemicals, for instance—to create experiences of this type.

Exposure to a memetic entity on the scale of Atem, one that is larger than the individual consciousness and that has the potential to overwhelm perception with novel and exciting experience, can also induce neuroplasticity. The method of full access to Atem includes exercises that involve new ways of experiencing, often with a physical component. Practicing the exercises can stimulate neuroplasticity as a regular and ongoing process. The individual human can then be open to really learning what the memetic entities have to teach.

Transformation

There are many different kinds and examples of *transformation*. There is the transformation that happens when someone is able to think about something in a different way. There is the transformation that takes place when a problem can be redefined to become an advantage. There is also the transformation of an individual consciousness, human or entity, when thought patterns are systematically and completely altered.

Long-term exposure to Atem or short-term exposure to an extremely powerful Atem-related experience can initiate a sweeping reorganization of the mind of an individual. By maintaining neuroplasticity over a long period of time, a human may be able to remap large parts of his or her consciousness.

In some human cultures, rites of passage mark some of the transitions a person can make in his or her life. These rites include powerful experiences of fear, disorientation, uncertainty, ecstasy, and so forth to create a sense of death and rebirth—and neuroplasticity. The old personality or internal construct dies and a newly organized consciousness can emerge. Neuroplasticity allows the changes to occur, but *transformation* describes the content and structure of the new neural pathways.

The content and structure described in this book can include the acquisition of these Eight Powers.

Transmission

Transmission is what makes a memetic entity "memetic." In the simple evocation exercises in this book, entities are delineated that may have no power of transmission. They appear, reveal their information, heal their subject, or perform their function, and then they are gone. A memetic entity, however, has the ability to spread through the noosphere from one mind to another, expanding and including more and more humans and entities whenever possible.

The most common modes of transmission are through language and media. This book is an example of how language and the industry of publishing can serve to transmit an entity. Transmission may also occur through practice groups, teaching, music, fiction, cinema, video, word of mouth, advertising, sculpture, painting, architecture and construction, and more. The media exist independently of transmission as the route of transmission. Something may appear in the media and then disappear again without ever transmitting itself. Atem, however, confers the ability to draw the attention of more and more individuals, providing them with enough benefit that a symbiotic relationship is established. It becomes appealing in various ways for a human to transmit Atem or another entity created with the help of Atem.

By offering the power of transmission to initiates, Atem gives them the ability to figure out how their work or the entities they create may fit with their target audience and what will induce transmission among that audience. This is an essential ability toward the spread of new or significant ideas, the growth of businesses, societal changes of various types, and the continuance of fictional characters and premises. Receiving the power of transmission itself may be sufficient inducement for many humans or entities to further transmit Atem.

Beauty

Beauty depends in large part on the elements of fitting and passion. We can identify beauty using the submodalities of perception. We then have the freedom to create works that match those particular submodalities, and we also have the ability to lead into more intense and novel beautiful experiences. The depth of understanding of the qualities of beauty is paired with the richness of the creations it inspires.

What are the submodalities in internal representation that someone associates with beauty? What physiological changes in the moment happen when beauty is experienced? What changes in the aura? By fitting with the structure of perception in this way, even the most novel kinds of beauty may be appreciated.

For something to be beautiful, to be aesthetically pleasing, a certain amount of congruence is necessary. Each part of the creation must fit with the whole. It must, in some way, convey the passion of the creator and must stimulate the passion of the audience.

Atem can access beauty in a number of ways. As an entity that spans multiple minds, he can offer broader perspectives, content that derives from the greater unconscious realms, and the aid of other entities who can act as muses or may offer technical information about particular media.

While beauty may often influence transmission, Atem ultimately hopes that beauty will be created for its own sake.

Understanding

Understanding is the ability to let experience find useful expression. A human or entity can absorb large amounts of information on a variety of levels. There is information on the level of content—what, specifically, we perceive. There is information on the level of structure—how and in what form we perceive. There is information on the level of the individual human and on the level of the multihuman entity. There is information on the level of the memetic entity and on the level of all entities, all consciousness. There is information on the level of the *whole.*

Specific elements of sensory information, the content of what we experience, will always presuppose the greater levels, up to the whole. And the greater levels will not only include the specific, but will also have similarity of structure to the specific, repeated again and again. It is from this continuum that all entities and humans and all parts of consciousness, internal and external, are delineated.

The individual human is often challenged to gain meaning from this macrocosmic fractal swirl. The conscious mind of the human is tiny, relative to the vastness of consciousness at large. It does not have the memory or processing ability to map even a small portion of the vastness. And yet the conscious mind itself does presuppose the greater consciousness. The trick is decoding the presuppositions.

If you read the section on language, you will have already had an experience of your own conscious mind decoding presuppositions. The examples given were small presuppositions, yet each took a measurable amount of time to bring into awareness. How much time would it take you to work out all the presupposed information in a volume of Shakespeare? How much time to work out the implicit world of the greater consciousness? How do you derive anything useful from so imposing a flow of experience?

The secret to understanding on levels beyond the human is simply to let larger entities do the processing work or to let your answers come from the whole.

Balance

Although the potential for *balance* exists everywhere and in everything, it is not inherent in the way we perceive things.

For a system to function for any amount of time, the parts must work in a harmonious way, each one fitting properly with the others. Each part may be doing a different job, but each is working toward the common goal, the specific function of the system. Think about how a human walks. Standing erect on two legs, the human must always maintain balance or run the risk of falling over. Maintaining that balance while moving, walking, running, carrying is not the job of any one part of the body. You don't maintain your balance by using only your arms or only your legs. You remain upright as the result of a complex interaction between many different muscles throughout the body. Each muscle is doing a different job, but each works toward the common goal of locomotion.

Likewise, the parts of consciousness involved in creating a memetic entity must work together in a way that benefits the specific purpose of the entity. This cooperation may often occur as a by-product of passion, or it may be thoroughly planned, in minute detail, in advance. Either way, Atem is frequently able to draw the individual's attention to situations requiring balance and to offer understanding of how balance may be achieved.

The power of balance is significantly useful among the eight powers. Creating balanced systems or balancing existing systems can result in increased efficiency, spontaneous healing of individuals, resolution of long-standing problems, innovation of various sorts, and much more.

Opening

Opening is the power to shift attention between parts of consciousness and to apprehend entities of many different types. This is the core of what Atem offers, the set of techniques and abilities that allow for the creation of and communication with entities.

When it is understood that our world as we perceive it is pure consciousness, then the way becomes open for a variety of phenomena. In short, the door to exploration of the greater consciousness is opened. Entities can then be delineated in numerous ways. Some of these may be strictly personal, operating within the limits of a single human, on the level of a psychological complex, imaginary friend, or recalled construct of someone once known. Others may be vast and world-spanning, such as the memetic entities that we call religions, systems of government, or corporations.

These encounters require effort that is commensurate with the scope and aims of the entities involved. The simple evocations of personal entities may require only a few moments of thought to accomplish. The creation of a world-spanning memetic entity may require years of preparation and organization. These are not, however, absolute; sometimes a moment's inspiration will create the most significant entities, or, conversely, the creation of a personal entity may involve considerable time and patience.

By reading this far, the way is already opening. Are you ready to explore?

SECOND INVOCATION OF ATEM

0. Find some time and space to be alone and uninterrupted for a little while. Turn off phones, computers, or any other possible distractions. This invocation can be performed with eyes open or closed, whichever is easiest for you. You can also choose to turn physically to face each direction, as necessary, or remain still, turning your attention to different directions.

1. Imagine a circle around you at a distance greater than arms' length. Choose six points that are spaced equidistant from each other on the circle.

2. Take a moment to recall a time when your field of **attention** was increased or modified in a powerful or enjoyable way. Remember this event as if you were another person, an observer, so that you see, hear, or feel yourself as if you were someone watching you. Examples of this kind of event include when the lights came on and you found your friends waiting for a surprise party; or you came up over a mountain, and suddenly a magnificent view opened up; or you were listening to music and had an epiphany about how the elements of music worked together; or your lover did something very different, and your physical awareness opened in a new way.

3. Place the images, sounds, and feelings of this experience of widened attention on one of the six points on the circle.

4. Think about a time when you either used **language** in a powerful and wonderful way or you were in awe by someone else's use of language. Again, remember this as if you were an observer.

5. Place the images, sounds, and feelings of this experience of language on the next of the six points on the circle, proceeding clockwise from the attention point.

6. Think of when you were totally engrossed in an amazing, enjoyable experience. Again, remember this experience of **passion** in a way that allows you to see, hear, or feel yourself as if you were another person.

7. Place the images, sounds, and feelings of this experience of passion on the next of the six points on the circle, proceeding clockwise from the language point.

8. Recall an experience when **fitting** was very easy and effective. For example, when you met someone new and kept finding out that you had more and more in common, or when you watched someone else easily fit in with a group of people he or she had never met before. Recall this in a way that allows you to observe yourself.

9. Place the images, sounds, and feelings of this experience of fitting on the next of the points of the circle, proceeding clockwise from the passion point.

10. Remember a time when you were in an interesting and enjoyable **trance**— relaxed in bed on a Sunday morning, while in a flow state, involved in meditation or hypnosis, or exploring consciousness in a significant way. See, hear, and/or feel as an observer.

11. Place the images, sounds, and feelings of this experience of trance on the next of the points of the circle, proceeding clockwise from the fitting point.

12. Think of a time when you had just completed **making** something that was significant in your life. For example, you finished a major project, put the finishing touches on a work of art, or just had a baby. Again, see, hear, or feel yourself as if you were someone else.

13. Place the images, sounds, and feelings of this experience of making on the last point on the circle.

14. Standing in the center of the circle, facing the direction you were originally facing, take one large step backwards.

15. Imagine that each of the qualities positioned around the circle is stretching out a tendril, a long strand of itself, toward the center of the circle, where you previously were standing.

16. Let the qualities meet in the center. Take a deep breath, and draw each of the qualities fully into the center, so that they all mingle together.

Watch, listen, and feel as they mingle. Notice what shapes this process takes, what it looks like or sounds like or feels like. Notice if it changes colors, or changes tones or texture, or any other way it responds as it fully joins together into one thing in the center of the circle.

17. Notice this shape, whatever it is. Look at it. Listen to it. Touch it.
18. Take a large step forward into the center of the circle, absorbing the shape into you.
19. In a loud, clear voice, say, **Atem.**
20. Remain silent and still for at least a few minutes as you take notice of whatever may result from your actions. See, hear, and feel whatever it is that you see, hear, and feel now.
21. Absorb any other imaginings from this ritual back into yourself, including the circle itself.

OPENING THE WAY

1. In a loud, clear voice, say, **Atem.**
2. Recall a time when you were in a significant altered state of consciousness. This could be a dream state; hypnogogic state; a state of deep relaxation; a state resulting from hypnosis, meditation, ritual, drumming, chanting, music, dancing, a psychoactive plant or chemical, sex; or anything that was enjoyable, educational, surreal, or somehow considered by you to be significant. Recall this from the point of view from which you originally experienced it, seeing, hearing, feeling, tasting, and smelling with your own sensory equipment.
3. Observe how your memory is represented. Is it primarily visual, auditory, or kinesthetic? Notice the structure of this memory, as well as the content. If you were remembering an evening spent in a relaxing hot tub, the *content* might include such things as the geographical location of the tub ("in the pool house, next to the sauna"), the size and color of the tub, and the temperature of the water. The *structure* of the memory would be where in the mental space around you, in your aura, you place the pictures, sounds, and feelings of the experience, how much space those representations occupy, and so on.
4. Breathe deeply and allow the representations of you memory to expand until they are at least life-sized (or as close as you can get—practice makes this easier). If by making them larger than life-sized, you continue to increase the intensity of the altered state, then continue to do so. Ideally, the image can surround you 360 degrees.
5. Give the experience a name—one word, whatever comes to mind first.

6. Enjoy the altered state for at least thirty seconds, then absorb all images, sounds, feelings, tastes, and smells back into you. Take a deep breath and stretch to break the state.

7. Repeat two more times, using memories of different altered states.

8. Say the three names rapidly in order. Do this six times.

9. In a loud, clear voice, say **Atem.**

SIMPLE EVOCATIONS

Basic Positive Resource Entity

1. **Banishing:** Imagine a circle around where you sit. Take a deep breath. As you inhale, let your awareness fill the circle. As you exhale, let your awareness contract to as small a point as you can, in the center of your chest. After five or six cycles of this, take a really, really, really deep breath, filling the circle with your awareness, then exhale forcefully and fully, letting your breath sweep through your personal circle, chasing out anything contrary to your purpose.

2. **Evocation:** Identify something in your life that makes you feel very good in some way. It can be a feeling of confidence, intelligence, satisfaction, arousal, intoxication, approval, or whatever you might describe as a good feeling. Pay very careful attention to *how* you feel, the structure of the feeling. Where does the feeling start? What kind of feeling is it? Where does it go as it develops? Does it continue to move? Is it static? Follow the feeling through to its peak. Then ask yourself, "If this feeling had a color, what would it be?" Imagine the color (or colors) in your body in exactly the areas where the feeling is experienced. Then imagine that you are taking the colored shape out of your body and flip it around to face you. Place it on the floor outside your circle and breathe deeply, feeding the shape breath and energy on each exhalation.

    Keep breathing and feeding it energy until it transforms. Once it has transformed, imagine you are communicating with it. Ask it what it wants to be called. Ask it what it can teach you that it has never before revealed. Ask it how you can feel really good more often. Find out whatever you can from it. Thank it for everything.

You can also ask this entity if it has anything that it would like to do away from your physical body, off in the external parts of consciousness. If it says that it does, then you can get an agreement of time from the entity—five minutes, an hour, a day, five years, or whatever time is appropriate to the task—and the promise from the entity to return to your physical presence at that time. Note down the time of the entity's return so that you can take notice when it occurs.

3. **Closing:** Reabsorb the entity and anything else you may have created in your aura during this operation.
4. Repeat **Banishing.**

Transforming Negative Entities

1. **Banishing:** Imagine a circle around where you sit. Take a deep breath. As you inhale, let your awareness fill the circle. As you exhale, let your awareness contract to as small a point as you can, in the center of your chest. After five or six cycles of this, take a really, really, really deep breath, filling the circle with your awareness, then exhale forcefully and fully, letting your breath sweep through your personal circle and chase out anything contrary to your purpose.
2. **Evocation:** Identify something in your life that makes you feel bad in some way. This technique can be used even with major trauma. It is recommended, however, that you begin with less intense experiences until you develop proficiency. For your first time, think about something in your life that is mildly unpleasant—a situation with family members or coworkers that leaves you feeling annoyed, for instance.

Again, notice where the feeling flows in your body and mark it out with colors as you did for the good feeling in the "Basic Positive Resource Entity" exercise. Flip the shape around and place it outside the circle, in front of you, but this time trap it in a geometric shape of some kind, such as a triangle or square drawn (in your imagination) on the floor.

Keep breathing and feeding it energy until it transforms. Once it has transformed, imagine you are communicating with it. Ask it what it wants to be called. Ask what it wants. Ask if there's a way for it to accomplish its goal in a more pleasant manner. Negotiate. Find out what it can do for you that it hasn't done before. Find out what you can do for it.

Keep breathing to feed it energy. It may transform again, if your negotiation is successful. If it does, flip it back around and draw it back into your body, in its original position.

If it doesn't change again, you have a couple of choices: (1) draw it back into yourself, but reversed from its original position, or (2) breathe and draw some energy from it with your inhalation until it has diminished somewhat, then reabsorb it back, flipped around, to its original position.

3.   Repeat **Banishing.**

Simple Entities, Around the Clock

The human organism and psyche exhibit rhythms of various kinds. Circadian rhythms rise and fall throughout the day, determining the variety of states that you pass through from waking to sleeping and everything in between. Ultradian rhythms rise and fall over a shorter period of time, accounting for changes in state by the minute or hour. Each of these states can be expressed as an entity. Very simply, at any given time you can ask, "How do I feel now?" If you carry out an evocation, as in the "Basic Positive Resource Entity" exercise, you can eventually collect a catalog of personal entities, each representing a particular time of the day.

Is the 2 P.M. Saturday entity the same as the 2 P.M. Thursday entity? Is the Tuesday 3:45 entity significantly different from the Tuesday 3:46 entity? Only you can answer these questions for yourself. Choosing a regular series of times when you perform such evocations will allow you to learn more about the habits and behavior of the many entities on your daily clock. There are many unique and exciting abilities conferred by this exercise.

Ultimately, this is an exercise in fitting with your own life.

Purposeful Entities

0. **Select** some single task that you wish to have accomplished. Phrase this task as a positive statement; "I want to stop feeling bad" or "I don't want chicken for dinner" are negative statements. They describe what is not wanted rather than what is wanted. "I want to feel good" or "I want spaghetti and meatballs for dinner" are positive statements. They describe what you want.
1. **Banish** as practiced in other evocations.
2. **Create a picture,** or an otherwise detailed description, in your mind of the task you chose, already accomplished. If you want to feel good, make an image or description of you already feeling good. If you want chicken for dinner, make an image or description of the ideal chicken dinner.
3. **Notice** what feelings are generated by imagining or describing this outcome. Continue to add sensory details to intensify the feelings. Make the feelings as strong as you are able.
4. **Use these feelings to evoke** an entity as practiced in other evocations.
5. **Communicate** with the entity to learn how your task can be accomplished. Find out how the entity will work (away from your physical presence, as part of you, by appearing at particular times or in specific circumstances, for example). Find out what you can do consciously to help obtain your outcome. Find out what consequent changes in your life this accomplishment will engender.
6. **Absorb** the entity and all pictures and descriptions back into you.
7. **Banish.**

Two Kinds of Entity Talismans

TALISMAN 1

1. **Banish.**
2. **Evoke** any kind of entity using the methods described so far: feelings converted to colored shapes and then externalized.
3. Using any kind of artistic medium that is appropriate, **draw** the shape that you have imagined for the externalized entity.
4. When your drawing is complete, **absorb** the entity back into you.
5. **Banish.**
6. The drawing of the entity can be used in any number of ways. For example, you can display it in a particular place that would benefit from the influence of that entity, carry it in your pocket, contemplate it at various times, or mail it to someone who might benefit from its presence.

TALISMAN 2

1. **Banish.**
2. **Evoke** any kind of entity using the methods described so far.
3. **Place an appropriate object** or symbol into the place where the entity has been evoked. The object can be chosen by several methods and can also represent the desired outcome in some way. For instance, a coin or bill or credit card might be used for an entity related to money, a leaf or flower or twig might be used for an outcome related to gardening or farming, a piece of jewelry with a particular stone or symbol might relate to a specific outcome, or you might create an appropriate sigil or symbol.
4. **Consult with the entity** as to how its essence can be applied to the object. If the entity does not know or doesn't respond clearly at first, you can offer choices: rub some of the visualized color onto the object; condense the entire shape, the entire entity, onto the object; allow it to climb inside the object if the object is suited for that; or simply have the object in the presence of the entity for a specific length of time.

5. **Apply the essence** of the entity to the object as decided above.
6. **Absorb** any remaining parts of the entity into yourself.
7. **Banish.**
8. The talisman can then be used in a way that fits with its purpose. The money can be spent or saved with other money. The leaf can be saved or placed in the garden. The jewelry can be worn, given to another person, or saved in a special place. The sigil or symbol can be contemplated, saved, destroyed, or whatever is appropriate.

Entities and Oracles

Oracles are entities that offer access to information that may be located in parts of consciousness that are not ordinarily accessible to the conscious mind. There are many different kinds of traditional oracle systems, including tarot cards, the I Ching, geomancy, and runes. Each of these systems in some way reflects a whole—either a whole consciousness or the whole universe. A randomizing act arranges the elements of this whole into different configurations for interpretation. Not only does each of these systems constitute a memetic entity in itself, in some of these systems, an entity was traditionally set over the operation to guide the oracle.

Similarly, the human organism, which reflects a whole, can operate with some of its parts outside of consciousness. In this way, the class of movements known as *ideomotor response* can be observed. Ideomotor response includes such phenomena as the use of a pendulum for dowsing, arm levitation in hypnosis, automatic writing, and kinesiological muscle testing, each of which can be used in oracular ways. A part of consciousness can be addressed as an entity—the unconscious mind, the part that wants to change, the creative part, the inner child, the totem spirit, whatever can be imagined—and the answers can be received via the unconscious movements of the ideomotor response. The pendulum will swing yes or no, the arm will raise or lower, the writing hand will elaborate, and the muscle tests will give both yes/no and qualitative responses.

By first evoking a particular entity and setting it to work over either a traditional oracle or an ideomotor technique, specific information can be accessed. If you want information about your love life, then evoke love as a purposeful entity and ask it to guide your tarot cards. If you want to learn about your financial decisions, evoke your feelings about money and then put it in charge of your pendulum hand. If you want to learn about evocation, then evoke Atem and ask him to guide your I Ching coins. Use any combination of entity and oracle that is appropriate for your purpose.

Possession

It is recommended that at least two people participate in this exercise. Both will help to evoke the entity, and one will become temporarily possessed.

1. **Banish.**
2. **Decide** on an entity to evoke.
3. **Evoke** an entity by one of the means described in the previous evocation exercises and hold it in a geometric shape. Both participants can do this simultaneously, but without sharing details. Both can observe how the energy and actions of the other influence what they are doing. The combined energies in the geometric shape may change or flow in unique ways.
4. The person to become possessed **enters the geometric shape** and either sits or stands in the same place as the entity. He or she sits quietly and becomes as receptive as possible until possession occurs. The other person can continue to breathe and feed energy to the entity throughout.
5. The person outside the shape can **ask questions** and converse with the entity through the possessed individual, depending on the nature of the entity. The possessed person may converse, describe an internal experience, or take action in a variety of ways. He or she should be encouraged to remain within the geometric shape throughout the experience.
6. When the experience is to end, the person leaves the geometric shape, being careful to **leave the entity behind.**

7. **Each participant reabsorbs** exactly as much attention as he or she contributed to the entity.
8. **Banish.**

Cloning Entities

Simple entities based on kinesthetic flows can be cloned in several ways:

- **Sit next to another person.** As you begin an evocation, noticing where feelings begin and where they flow to, use descriptive language to teach this flow to the other person. Identify out loud what kinds of feelings are involved (such as temperature, pressure, movement, tingling, or bubbling). Identify where and when the feelings move. Continue the description up to and including the peak of the experience. Then both participants can use that kinesthetic flow to evoke the same entity. This evocation can also be accomplished by teaching a flow to a group, all at once. If passed along from person to person in this way, repeatedly, some loss or distortion of information will occur and clones may mutate.
- **Evoke an entity before you.** Then, leaving the entity in external consciousness, reinitiate the flow in yourself. Evoke the second (or third, fourth, fifth) flow into a second entity. Some minor variations may occur.
- **Evoke an entity before you.** Explain to the entity your need for a clone and ask it to divide. If a need is present, most entities of this sort can divide into at least several clones with no variation or mutation.

Accessing Existing Entities

Evocation techniques of many kinds have developed throughout human history, and quite a bit of information about specific historical entities is easily obtainable. This includes detailed records of simple evocations in classic grimoires, accounts of deities and pantheons from every culture, mythic and fictional entities of every type, as well as larger memetic entities such as languages, religions, epistemologies, political systems, economic systems, and so on. Even the most complex of these entities can be at least partially accessed using the following simple evocation technique:

1. **Banish.**
2. **Contemplate** what you know about the entity. If it has visible manifestations, visualize these, if it has audible aspects, hear those, and allow whatever feelings these images and sounds produce to build in you.
3. **Use the flow of feelings to evoke** the entity.
4. **Conduct your business** with the entity.
5. **Banish.**

Entity Groups

Sometimes it is useful to evoke multiple entities simultaneously. A group of entities has advantages in terms of flexibility and utility. The entities can do more, and they can act independently of each other and in synchronization when necessary.

The group of entities itself can embody information in a variety of ways, including the number of entities involved, the shape in which they are evoked and maintained, and the degree of polarity or complementariness between the entities. Numbers and shapes have symbolic value; these can be chosen based on the task at hand. The relationships between the entities can also be charged with meaning in a variety of ways. As an obvious example, an entity representing male sexual interest would interact with an entity representing female sexual interest in a different way that it would an entity that represents computer programming.

An entity based on fire would relate differently to entities based on water or wood. Designing the shapes and interactions of entity groups is an art in itself.

These groups of entities can be evoked to act as protectors, provide information, offer motivation, or fill any number of other roles.

The "Second Invocation of Atem," described earlier, is an example of an entity group based on the six elements of Atem. Entities representing Attention, Language, Passion, Fitting, Trance, and Making are arranged symmetrically around a circle, and then merged together.

Group Entities

Simple evocations can be practiced with groups of any size. It requires only an agreement of cooperation and a willingness to recognize and appreciate the different perspective of each human.

1. **The members of the group sit in a circle,** facing inward. A quality to evoke will be agreed upon—for instance, "prosperity," "wisdom," or any quality the group decides will be useful for everyone.
2. **Banish.** Each person, simultaneously, will breathe and banish as in previous evocations, using the entire group circle as the space within which to expand and contract attention.
3. **A geometric shape is drawn** or imagined by everyone on the floor in the center of the circle—for instance, a triangle or square.
4. **Each person will perform a simple evocation** of the kind described in the "Basic Positive Resource Entity" exercise, based on the previously decided quality. For example, each person will think about what "prosperity" means to him or her—what it might look like, what it might sound like, feel like, taste like, and smell like. The feeling that develops becomes the basis for the entity.
5. **Each individual entity is then placed in the center** of the circle, inside the geometric shape drawn or imagined on the floor. The entities are allowed to merge together in whatever way they do.
6. **Each person communicates with the collective entity** in whatever way he or she has decided on or may choose.

7. When everyone has satisfactorily finished communication with the entity, or at an agreed-upon time, **each person then absorbs back into him- or herself exactly as much energy as he or she initially gave forth.**
8. **Banish.**

Destruction of Entities

Destruction of entities is only rarely useful. Most often, simple entities are parts of your own consciousness. They are composed of your own attention. If problems are associated with an entity, transformation is usually more desirable than destruction. That way, you have lost nothing of yourself, but rather have aligned it to be in harmony with the rest of your consciousness. Once in a great while, though, an entity is purely unnecessary and a hindrance, and the most expedient method of dealing with it is simply to be rid of it.

Once an entity has been called into being, it is nearly impossible to destroy entirely. As long as some memory of the entity remains in the mind of any human, the entity will still exist in some fashion. However, for practical purposes, it is possible to effect near-total destruction of simple entities. It is much more difficult, although still possible, to wipe out a larger memetic entity.

The following techniques apply to simple entities:

- **Give the entity a symbolic finish.** It can be devoured by a larger entity. It can be trapped in a talisman that is then destroyed in some way—burned, flushed, buried, or eaten, for example. The entity can be tossed into the sun or into the molten core of the Earth. A quality can be added to it that rots it, burns it, or evaporates it.
- **Remove attention from the entity**—essentially forgetting it. As long as the entity receives attention of any kind, it exists. When attention is removed, it becomes dormant. When thought of the particular entity begins to arise, the attention is turned elsewhere, preferably to something even more engrossing. If hypnosis or neurolinguistic techniques

are known, they may help by using anchors to change states, induce amnesia, or associate a different or altered flow of feelings with the entity.

- **Dissolve the entity** back into undifferentiated consciousness. Inhale it or exhale it, and imagine the entity dispersing, its components becoming part of everything around it.

PART TWO
Thirty-six Days of Atem

INTRODUCTION

THE FOLLOWING PAGES DESCRIBE an experiential exploration of the Six Elements of Atem. An exercise or set of exercises is offered for each of thirty-six days. It is recommended that these exercises be practiced completely, in the order given, for that period of time. If a day must be missed here or there due to circumstances, then pick up again with the next exercise in sequence. Do them all!

Some of these exercises may be familiar to you from other fields of study, including martial arts, meditation, neurolinguistic programming, hypnosis, or ritual practice. Most of these have been modified in some way from their original influences. If you think you have previously practiced an exercise exactly as given, that will be an asset to you. You can benefit most from this system if you do the exercise again when it falls in the sequence. There are elements of context and sequence that make the entirety of the Thirty-six Days of Atem a unique experience. Each exercise fits in with the others in a way that helps to activate the mind of Atem in the realm of your own consciousness and gives you access to, among other things, the Eight Powers of Atem. Do all of the exercises!

Some of the exercises require a partner to practice. If necessary, you may adapt these for solo practice when possible. However, initial practice with a partner will most often provide the best results. Better yet, the exercises can be explored in the context of a practice group where the exercises and results are enhanced by the presence of and interaction with a variety of personalities, tendencies, and levels of experience. In the case of a practice group that may be able to meet weekly or monthly, the thirty-six-day format and order of the exercises may be modified in a variety of ways.

DAY ONE: ATTENTION/ATTENTION

HOW WE DIRECT OUR ATTENTION can determine our present experience. This principle can be tested experimentally in a variety of ways. The following three exercises demonstrate how simple changes in attention engender changes in the external consciousness.

Forward/Backward Thinking

1. Person A holds out an arm, fully extended, palm facing forward. Person B holds hands up in front of his or her chest, at the level of Person A's arm. (See fig. A.)

2. Person B walks forward at an even pace and continues on even after contacting Person A's arm. Person B calibrates, learning how much effort is necessary to walk past Person A's arm.

Figure A

3. Participants return to their original positions. Person B picks an object or location some distance *ahead* of him- or herself. B continues to think about that object or location as he or she, again, presses past Person A's arm. B notes how much effort is necessary to walk past A's arm with attention *ahead*.

4. Participants return to their original positions. Person B picks an object or location some distance *behind* him- or herself. B continues to think

about that object or location as he or she, again, presses past Person A's arm. B notes how much effort is necessary to walk past A's arm with attention *behind*.

5. Partners switch positions and repeat steps 1 through 4.

6. Partners take a few moments to discuss their observations.

Up/Down Thinking

This exercise is performed by three people.

1. Person A stands in the center, and B and C take positions on either side, facing A. Person A holds elbows at sides, forearms folded up against upper arms. B and C take hold of A's elbows. (See fig. B.)

2. B and C carefully lift A, calibrating and learning how much effort is needed to lift Person A in this manner. A is then gently lowered back to the floor.

3. Person A thinks about something *up above* him- or herself. The more distant this object or location is, the better. Clouds or a distant star are ideal. While A continues to direct attention *up*, B and C carefully lift A. B and C take note

Figure B

how much effort is needed to lift A while he or she is directing attention *up*.

4. Person A thinks about something *below* him- or herself. The more distant this object or location is, the better. The center of the Earth is ideal. While A continues to direct attention *down*, B and C carefully lift A. B and C take note how much effort is needed to lift A while he or she is directing attention *down*.

5. Participants take a few moments to discuss their observations.

Circular Thinking

This exercise normally requires at least two people. One will perform the experiment while the partner(s) will observe as closely as possible. A solo version can be performed using a video-recording device as an observer.

1. Person A imagines a circle drawn around him or her on the floor. He or she stands in the exact center of the circle, making sure that the circumference is an equal distance in front of him or her as it is behind, and is an equal distance to the right as it is to the left.
2. A imagines that the circle is sliding forward along the floor, until it has moved, in its entirety, in front of A. A holds this imagining for a moment, then returns the circle to its original position.
3. A imagines that the circle is sliding backward along the floor, until it has moved, in its entirety, behind A. A holds this imagining for a moment, then returns the circle to its original position.
4. A imagines that the circle is sliding to the right along the floor, until it has moved, in its entirety, to the right of A. A holds this imagining for a moment, then returns the circle to its original position.
5. A imagines that the circle is sliding to the left along the floor, until it has moved, in its entirety, to the left of A. A holds this imagining for a moment, then returns the circle to its original position.
6. Observers discuss what they observed, no matter how minute.
7. Person A discusses what the experience was like from his or her point of view.
8. Participants change positions and repeat the experiment, rotating until everyone has served as both observer and observed.

DAY TWO: ATTENTION/LANGUAGE

BY DESCRIBING OR DIRECTING OUR ATTENTION with language, we can create very specific and subtle distinctions. While we may often think of language as being strictly spoken or written, the content of language encompasses all the senses.

What Sense?

1. Work in pairs. Person A asks Person B general questions about familiar things, such as, "What do you like best about where you live?" "What do you like best about the place where we are now?" "What do you remember most from last year?" Notice that none of these questions include any reference to a particular sense and are as open ended as possible. "Where you live" is less specific than "your house," for instance. Someone might not live in a house. He or she might live in an apartment or a yurt.

2. Person A pays careful attention to Person B's responses to the questions, listening closely for sense-related words (see appendix C). Verbs and adjectives in the sentence will relate to a particular sense. Person A identifies if Person B is processing perceptions through the visual, kinesthetic, auditory, gustatory, or olfactory sense. For example:
    A: What do you like best about the place where you live?
    B: The **view** is wonderful. (Visual)
    A: What do you like best about the place where we are now?

B: It's very **comfortable.** (Kinesthetic feeling)

A: What do you remember most from last year?

B: I remember **hearing** that new CD for the first time. (Auditory)

If the answer includes unspecified words, then Person A continues to ask questions until the senses involved are revealed.

A: What do you like best about the place where you live?

B: It's so nice.

A: What's nice about it?

B: I just like it.

A: What exactly do you like about it?

B: Just **looking** at the big trees on the property.

3. Person A repeats the information back to B using different sense words.

   B: I like how **quiet** it is.

   A: You like it because it **looks** peaceful.

4. Person A repeats the information back to B, using the same sense words.

   B: I like how **quiet** it is.

   A: You like it because it is **quiet.**

5. B notes any subjective response to the changes in sense words, as A speaks.

6. A and B take a few moments to discuss what happened.

7. Partners switch positions and repeat the exercise.

DAY THREE: ATTENTION/PASSION

BREATH IS VERY DIRECTLY ENERGIZING TO BODY AND MIND. There's nothing mystical about it; the body relies on the presence of oxygen to function and responds physiologically in different ways to different amounts of gases in the system. As well, breath is a direct link to the unconscious mind. Breathing is a behavior that is usually outside of awareness when we turn our attention toward the external consciousness, and when we do turn our attention to breathing, it quickly falls under conscious control.

Expansion and Contraction

1. Each person works alone. Sitting in a comfortable position with spine upright and straight, imagine a circle around you with a diameter just slightly greater than your outstretched arms, and you are in the exact center.
2. Inhale, filling your lungs completely, from bottom to top. As you inhale, allow your attention to expand to fill the circle. If it helps to imagine your aura as a particular color or glow that fills the circle, then add in that visualization.
3. Exhale completely. As you exhale, draw your attention in to a tiny spot within the center of your chest.
4. Repeat for at least ten minutes, filling the circle with every inhalation, contracting down to a single point in the center of your chest with every exhalation.

5. When you finish, remain in the same position and take a few moments to reflect on what you experienced.

Bigger Expansion

1. Perform the expansion and contraction exercise as above, but expand to fill a much greater area. This area should have definite boundaries. You could fill the room or the building that you are in. Then contract with your exhalation as in the previous exercise.
2. Repeat for at least five minutes.
3. When you finish, remain in the same position and take a few moments to reflect on what you experienced.

Biggest Expansion

1. Perform the expansion and contraction exercise as above, but expand to fill the greatest area that you can conceive of in your mind. Fill the world, or the solar system, or the galaxy, or the entire universe, if you can. Then contract with your exhalation as in the previous exercise.
2. Repeat for at least five minutes.
3. When you finish, remain in the same position and take a few moments to reflect on what you experienced.

DAY FOUR: ATTENTION/FITTING

THIS EXERCISE DEMONSTRATES THE IMPORTANCE OF FITTING in communication, transmission, and understanding.

Conversational Fitting

1. Partners sit next to each other. Person A asks Person B to tell something about his or her day, either something that has already happened or something that has yet to happen. Person B's speech should last two or three minutes.
2. As B speaks, A pays attention to the following:
    a. B's posture
    b. The rhythm of B's breathing (noticeable when he or she speaks —you can speak only as you exhale)
    c. Any gestures or movements that B makes
    d. All sensory-based words that B uses
3. While B is speaking, A makes his or her best effort to physically match B's posture, rhythm of breathing, and gestures or movements. Since this is a lot of information to process consciously, A should accomplish as much as his or her present ability allows.
4. When B has finished speaking, Person A tells B something about A's day, using the sensory terms that B has demonstrated and matching B's posture and rhythms as much as possible. If B told a story about hearing something wonderful, then A tells a similarly auditory-inclined story. A can feel free to use fictional details, if necessary.

5. When A has finished this story, the partners swap roles. Person A tells B something about A's day, in his or her own terms, and B does the matching and follow-up storytelling.
6. Partners take a few moments to discuss their experiences of this exercise.

DAY FIVE: ATTENTION/TRANCE

THIS EXERCISE DEMONSTRATES HOW THE STRUCTURE of our imagination creates our reality and also helps to develop evocation skills. As a solo practice, it can be a fast and useful way to relax in a variety of circumstances.

Watch Yourself Relax

1. Person A guides Person B through the following instructions:
   a. "Imagine that you can see yourself, or hear yourself, or feel yourself, as if observing another person. Make it like looking at a movie or a picture of yourself. If you are better at hearing or feeling, then hear yourself talking or making sounds, or feel where your presence would be.
   b. "Imagine that this other self that you are observing is in a place that is very comfortable and very, very relaxing. It's not necessary to see, hear, or feel the place; just keep your attention on this other self.
   c. "Watch, listen, and/or feel as this other self becomes more and more relaxed, more and more comfortable, and exhibits the effects of relaxation: softer muscles, different posture, different facial expression, and so forth."
2. Person A lightly takes hold of B's wrist and gently lifts B's arm up, continuing to talk about the image of the relaxed self. A instructs B to "just let the arm hang there in the air, just like that." (See fig. C.) If B's attention is properly directed toward the relaxed self image, the arm will stay in whatever position it is left.

3. A instructs B to "let your unconscious mind lower the arm only as fast as you become more relaxed, and allow it to rise with unconscious movements if you should become less relaxed."

4. A makes various suggestions to B to alter the latter's self-image and observes to see whether the arm raises or lowers. When the arm lowers, A increases those suggestions so that B's state of relaxation is increased as much as possible. Note that A's suggestions will relate to the structure of the visualization, rather than the content. For instance:
   - "Make the image larger or smaller."
   - "Make the colors brighter or more muted."
   - "Emphasize the foreground as opposed to the background," and vice versa.
   - "Make the sounds or speech louder or quieter" (if the emphasis is on hearing rather than seeing).
   - "Speed up and slow down the action" (works for all senses).
   - "Move the image closer or farther away" (works for all senses).
   - "Give the image a soft glow or sparkles."

5. When B's arm eventually comes all the way down to rest, A suggests that B enjoy the relaxed state for a few moments. B allows the self-image to disappear and takes a few more moments to return to normal consciousness, with the suggestion from A to feel refreshed and alert.

6. Partners then switch roles, and the experiment is repeated.

7. A and B take a few moments to discuss their experiences.

Figure C

DAY SIX: ATTENTION/MAKING

THIS EXERCISE IS PERFORMED BY EACH PERSON INDIVIDUALLY.

Attention Entity

1. Define a circle around you and perform expansion/contraction breaths while sitting or standing in the exact center. Inhale and expand your attention to fill the circle. Exhale and contract your attention to a single point in the center of your chest. Repeat at least three times.
2. Take notice of six points, placed equal distances apart, along the circumference of the circle.
3. Recall the experience of performing the Day One exercises, "Forward/Backward Thinking," "Up/Down Thinking," and "Circular Thinking." Think about what you saw as you practiced, what you heard, what you felt, and whether there were any notable tastes or smells. Whatever perceptual representations you make of these memories—whether they are images, sounds, voices, feelings, or tastes and smells, take a deep breath and project those representations into a sphere on one of the points on the circle. Take another deep breath and project the exhalation into the sphere.
4. Recall the experience of performing the Day Two exercise, "What Sense?," and then project whatever perceptual representations you make of this memory into a sphere on one of the points on the circle. Take another deep breath and project the breath into the sphere.
5. Recall the experience of performing the Day Three exercises, "Expansion and Contraction," "Bigger Expansion," and "Biggest Expansion,"

and then project whatever perceptual representations you make of these memories into a sphere on one of the points on the circle. Take another deep breath and project the breath into the sphere.

6. Recall the experience of performing the Day Four exercise, "Conversational Fitting," and then project whatever perceptual representations you make of this memory into a sphere on one of the points on the circle. Take another deep breath and project the breath into the sphere.

7. Recall the experience of performing the Day Five exercise, "Watch Yourself Relax," and then project whatever perceptual representations you make of this memory into a sphere on one of the points on the circle. Take another deep breath and project the breath into the sphere.

8. Take note of what you are doing now, the Day Six exercise, "Attention Entity," and then project whatever perceptual representations you make of this experience into a sphere on one of the points on the circle. Take another deep breath and project the breath into the sphere.

9. Take a step backward, leaving the center of the circle empty.

10. Take a deep breath and direct your exhalation into the center of the circle. As you do so, allow the six spheres to draw inward, combining into a single shape in the center of the circle. Allow that shape to take whatever form seems natural to it. Continue to breathe deeply and project your breath into the shape.

11. In your thoughts, communicate with the entity. Find out if there is a special name or symbol that it would like to use. Find out if it knows what you have learned about attention from these exercises. Find out what else it can teach you, right now or later, about attention.

12. Have it explain, or decide along with the entity, how to quickly and easily resummon the entity at a later date. That might involve recalling a particular sensory element, saying a particular word or name, or following a method of any kind. Take note of this information so that you can use it later.

13. When you are finished, take a deep breath and draw the entity, any remaining spheres, and the circle back into yourself.

14. Repeat the expansion/contraction breathing as in step 1.

15. Take a few moments to reflect on what you have experienced.

DAY SEVEN: LANGUAGE/LANGUAGE

IN ALL THE EXERCISES IT IS IMPORTANT for participants to recognize the wide variety of responses among different humans. There is really no one thing that makes something beautiful to everyone. We can, however, start to understand what makes things beautiful for the people around us. This exercise encourages neuroplasticity as well as communication and other powers.

Beautiful Language

1. Person A describes something that he or she perceives as "beautiful" to Person B.
2. B asks A questions to determine what it is about this thing that A finds beautiful. What are the qualities that make something beautiful for A? For instance:

   A: I think the sunset over the mountains is beautiful.

   B: What about it is beautiful?

   A: The colors, the shapes of the clouds, the rays of the sun.

   B: What is it about the colors that make it beautiful?

   A: I like those shades of red and gold.

   B: What is it about the shapes of the clouds that make it beautiful?

   A: They look like a field of cotton in the sky.
3. A and B both discuss these ideas and bring their attention to any presuppositions they might find in A's language. For instance:
   - There is something about red and gold that A likes.
   - Red and gold come in various shades.

- The clouds had a particular shape, and the sun shone through them.
- Fields of cotton look beautiful to A.

These presuppositions can be further explored. What is it about red and gold? What is it about a field of cotton?

4. B picks something within the present field of vision and makes suggestions to A to view it or experience it as beautiful, using whatever cues or criteria A may have described previously. For instance:
   B: Can you imagine that chair in shades of red and gold? What if the chair had a surface like a field of cotton?
   However A responds is fine.
5. Partners then switch roles and repeat the experiment.
6. A and B take a few moments to reflect and discuss their experiences.

DAY EIGHT: LANGUAGE/ATTENTION

WHERE YOU PUT YOUR ATTENTION at any given time is often partly uncconscious. Exploring with language can reveal information about what draws your attention and how the attention is used.

First Thing You See

1. Person A closes his or her eyes. A is then turned around several times by B and instructed to open his or her eyes. A takes note of the first thing that draws his or her attention—"the first thing you see." Alternatively, this could be done with earplugs, and A can note the first thing he or she hears. Or a variety of objects can be placed in a bag, and A can reach in and find the first thing he or she feels.

2. A describes that object or thing in purely sensory terms, without naming it and without giving names to component parts. For instance, if the object is a chair, it is described without mention of it being a chair and without terms like *back,* or *legs,* or *cushion.* A is also careful not to let physical cues—such as looking directly at the object, touching it, or pointing to it—tip off B as to what is being described. For example: A: Four metal columns touch the floor and rise up to support a platform. The platform has soft material on it a few inches thick. The material is blue, and the metal columns are gray. Attached perpendicular to the platform is a curved panel . . .

3. After A is allowed to make a full description, B attempts to guess the object. If incorrect, A continues the description until B is able to

guess correctly. If correct, B then offers any details, in sensory-based language, that A may have missed or described in a way that was confusing.

4. Partners switch roles and repeat the experiment.
5. A and B take a few moments to reflect and discuss their experiences.

DAY NINE: LANGUAGE/PASSION

THE ELEMENTS OF YOUR OWN AURA can be conveyed through language in ways that influence the auras of others. This exercise encourages the power of transmission.

Passionate Storytelling

1. Person A takes a few moments to recall a particularly enjoyable and engrossing experience. This could be from recent or past experience, as long as it can be recalled with detail. A remembers what that experience looked like from his or her point of view—what colors were present, what kind of movement or stillness were seen, what sounds could be heard, whether these were tones, voices, or something else, what tastes or smells were present, what could be felt, whether these feelings included temperature, posture, breathing, and as much additional detail as A can quickly and easily recall.
2. Person A uses spoken language to describe this experience to Person B, using tone of voice, posture, and mannerisms to convey the experience in as much detail as possible.
3. As Person A speaks, he or she observes Person B carefully, watching to see what kind of response B is having to the description of experience. A repeats and emphasizes the kinds of details that appear to bring B deeper into the experience.
4. After B appears to be satisfactorily enjoying the feeling of the experience for at least a minute or two, partners can switch roles and repeat the experiment.
5. Partners take a few moments to reflect and discuss the experience.

DAY TEN: LANGUAGE/FITTING

LANGUAGE CAN FIT INTO ANOTHER PERSON'S AURA VERY NEATLY, like a key into a lock. To fit effectively, there must be a feedback loop between the speaker and the listener and some way for the speaker to understand and match elements of the listener's aura.

Hearing Voices

1. Work in pairs. Person A identifies a particular voice that he or she finds motivating or exciting. This could be an internal voice that he or she experiences in certain situations—we all have certain things that we say to ourselves to motivate or excite ourselves—"Go for it!"; "All right!"; "Now we're talking!" This can be our own voice or that of someone we respect who provides motivation or excitement, such as a teacher, a coach, a lover, a friend, or a parent.
2. Person A describes what the voice says, what kind of voice it is (the volume, the tone, and the rhythm of the voice), where the voice seems to come from in the memory (where in A's aura it is located, rather than in the context of the memory), and anything else about the voice that is pertinent.
3. Person B imitates the voice as closely as possible. B positions his or her mouth in the place the voice seems to come from and matches volume, tone, rhythm, and the exact words of the voice.
4. Partners switch roles and repeat the experiment.
5. Partners take a few moments to reflect and discuss their experience.

DAY ELEVEN: LANGUAGE/TRANCE

TRANCE STATES CAN BE INDUCED by the language we encounter and can also be identified by the language we use. How much of our present experience is determined by other humans or by memetic entities?

Cultural Trances

1. Person A makes three statements about him- or herself. These statements can be anything as long as they are descriptive. They can be perceived as positive statements or negative statements. They can be perceived as self-supporting or self-deprecating.

2. Person B identifies any culturally derived presuppositions in the statements, or asks questions about them to discover if they are dependent on culturally derived presuppositions. For instance:

   A: I'm a lazy person.

   B: Lazy about what?

   A: I never do what I am supposed to do.

   B: What are you supposed to do?

   A: Get up early, get to work on time, pick up my socks.

   B: What makes you think you are supposed to do these things?

   A: My boss gets on my case if I'm late. My wife nags me about the socks.

   B: Cultural presuppositions I identify here include a work ethic—the idea that you must do what your boss tells you, that you must work at a job to be a good human. Also that you must "honor and obey" your wife.

3. Both partners consider these statements and decide whether or not they represent the ideas perpetuated by a memetic entity: a school of thought, a corporation, an ideology, a religion, a cultural institution, or a deity. In the above case, we might say "Puritan Work Ethic" and "Marriage" are possible names for entities involved. This process (steps 2 and 3) is repeated for each of the three statements.
4. Partners switch roles and repeat the exercise.
5. Partners take a few moments to reflect and discuss their experience.

DAY TWELVE: LANGUAGE/MAKING

THIS EXERCISE IS PERFORMED BY EACH PERSON INDIVIDUALLY.

Language Entity

1. Define a circle around you, and perform expansion/contraction breaths while sitting or standing in the exact center. Inhale and expand your attention to fill the circle. Exhale and contract your attention to a single point in the center of your chest. Repeat at least three times.
2. Take notice of six points, placed equal distances apart, along the circumference of the circle.
3. Recall the experience of performing the Day Seven exercise, "Beautiful Language." Think about what you saw as you practiced, what you heard, what you felt, and whether there were any notable tastes or smells. Whatever perceptual representations you make of this memory— whether they are images, sounds, voices, feelings, tastes, or smells— take a deep breath and project those representations into a sphere on one of the points on the circle. Take another deep breath and project the exhalation into the sphere.
4. Recall the experience of performing the Day Eight exercise, "First Thing You See," and then project whatever perceptual representations you make of this memory into a sphere on one of the points on the circle. Take another deep breath and project the breath into the sphere.
5. Recall the experience of performing the Day Nine exercise, "Passionate Storytelling," and then project whatever perceptual representations you

make of this memory into a sphere on one of the points on the circle. Take another deep breath and project the breath into the sphere.

6. Recall the experience of performing the Day Ten exercise, "Hearing Voices," and then project whatever perceptual representations you make of this memory into a sphere on one of the points on the circle. Take another deep breath and project the breath into the sphere.

7. Recall the experience of performing the Day Eleven exercise, "Cultural Trances," and then project whatever perceptual representations you make of this memory into a sphere on one of the points on the circle. Take another deep breath and project the breath into the sphere.

8. Take note of what you are doing now, the Day Twelve exercise, "Language Entity," and then project whatever perceptual representations you make of this experience into a sphere on one of the points on the circle. Take another deep breath and project the breath into the sphere.

9. Take a step backward, leaving the center of the circle empty.

10. Take a deep breath and direct your exhalation into the center of the circle. As you do so, allow the six spheres to draw inward, combining into a single shape in the center of the circle. Allow that shape to take whatever form seems natural to it. Continue to breathe deeply and project your breath into the shape.

11. In your thoughts, communicate with the entity. Find out if there is a special name or symbol that it would like to use. Find out if it knows what you have learned about language from these exercises. Find out what else it can teach you, right now or later, about language.

12. Have it explain, or decide along with the entity, how to quickly and easily resummon the entity at a later date. That might involve recalling a particular sensory element, saying a particular word or name, or following a method of any kind. Take note of this information so that you can use it later.

13. When you are finished, take a deep breath and draw the entity, any remaining spheres, and the circle back into yourself.

14. Repeat the expansion/contraction breathing as in step 1.

15. Take a few moments to reflect on what you have experienced.

DAY THIRTEEN: PASSION/PASSION

THERE ARE MANY DIFFERENT PRACTICAL USES for this exercise. Similar techniques in the fields of neurolinguistics and hypnosis are used in habit control, motivation, and changes in self-concept. The exercise is included here, however, as a means to increase congruence, which is applicable to the powers of transmission, transformation, beauty, understanding, and balance.

Increasing Passion

1. Person A thinks of two different situations in his or her life, one that is neutral—not particularly appealing, yet not particularly objectionable—and one that exemplifies passion.

2. A describes both of these memories as B observes and makes a mental map of A's representations. Does A represent these using primarily one sense or another? Are the representations close or far away? Are they still, or do they move? Person B can use the chart in appendix B to find categories of sensory submodalities to ask A about. This process yields two different maps: one of A's aura in a neutral situation and one of A's aura in a powerfully passionate situation.

3. B compares the two auras, paying attention to the differences in structure. Are the representations in different senses? Or are they in the same sense with different submodalities?

4. B guides A through a process of taking the aura of A's passionate experience and emphasizing whatever it is that makes it different from the "neutral aura." If the representations are in different senses, then

increase awareness of whatever sense the "passionate aura" is found in. If the neutral one is an image and the passionate-experience one is a feeling, then B works to make the feelings of that passionate experience more powerful. If both experiences are represented in the same sense, then B begins to emphasize whatever submodality differences are found; that is, if both experiences are image based, but the passionate-experience image is bigger, then B continues to make the passionate images bigger.

5. B continues until A's responses begin to drop off again; that is, if Person B is guiding A to make an image bigger, B observes A's responses as he or she provides guidance. A's responses will get stronger and stronger until they reach a threshold level, then will likely drop off. As soon as B notices the responses dropping back off, then he or she suggests to A that he or she reverses the process, now making the image smaller (or opposite of whatever was done).

6. When A has returned to something approximating his or her original state of consciousness, the partners switch roles and repeat the exercise.

7. Both partners take a few moments to reflect and discuss their experience.

DAY FOURTEEN: PASSION/ATTENTION

THE ELEMENTS OF A SINGLE HUMAN'S AURA constitute a reflection of the universe at large. Every conscious entity will have a similar structure, representing the whole. Working with these microcosmic structures encourages neuroplasticity, transformation, understanding, balance, and opening. Performing this exercise repeatedly, with many different people and different experiences, will maximize its effect. This exercise provides practice in increasing congruence.

Shifting Auras

1. Person A selects a powerful, passionate experience, as in the Day Thirteen "Increasing Passion" exercise.
2. Person B asks questions to determine what senses and submodalities of those senses are involved in A's experience.
3. With the understanding that A is just "trying these on," Person B guides A through a variety of reconfigurations of the structure of the experience. These can include:
    *   Changing the predominant senses. If A sees an image of the experience, then B can guide his or her attention predominantly to the auditory and kinesthetic portions of the experience.
    *   Changing the direction or location of the experience. B can suggest that A move the experience all in front, then to each side, then to the back. If the experience is predominantly an internal kinesthetic one, then B can help A move it through different areas of the body and different locations of the external consciousness as well, if A is able.

- Changing the size of the representations. B can suggest making them very, very small and then very, very big. If the experience is visual, changing the size of representations means changing the size of the image. If the experience is auditory, it means changing the size of the imagined source of the sound. If the experience is kinesthetic, it means having A feeling the experience through or over more of the body or in an area greater than the body.

4. Both partners observe which of these configurations are associated with increased and decreased response, whether or not each configuration is more or less easy to accomplish, whether each configuration tends to revert to a previous configuration or if it easily stays as positioned.

5. A is asked to decide which configuration he or she would like to keep, or if A would rather the configuration were returned to its original form. B then guides A through the process of creating whatever configuration A has chosen.

6. Partners switch roles and repeat the exercise.

7. Both partners take a few moments to reflect and discuss their experiences.

DAY FIFTEEN: PASSION/LANGUAGE

EXPLORING THE CLOUD OF SUBMODALITY DATA that defines a state can easily be a precursor to a full evocation. The information related to a single state, though it may be relatively small in quantity, implies a whole, a much larger set of data. The ability to communicate submodality information through language, in subtle ways, can be of enormous importance to the transmission of memetic entities.

The Story of Passion

1. Using what was learned about Person A (if with the same partner) in "Increasing Passion" (Day Thirteen) and "Shifting Auras" (Day Fourteen), Person B tells a story that elicits a powerful, passionate state in A. B attempts to incorporate all the sensory shifts that increased passionate experience in the previous two exercises. For instance, if A responded strongly to an increased image size, B might describe something as being on a really large movie screen, or some element in B's story gets larger and larger and larger. If A responded strongly to feelings of, for instance, tingling in the extremities, then B's story describes how someone experienced that exact kind of tingling.

    a. B tells the story without making direct reference to the previous exercises, but incorporating what was learned; that is, describe another experience entirely, and use the submodality language that A connects with increased passion.

b. B observes A closely as the story develops. If A's attention or level of response drops off, then B can use other submodality shifts. If A's attention and level of response continues to increase, then B can continue to work with those submodalities that are getting a good response.

c. B's story continues for no longer than ten minutes.

2. Partners switch roles and repeat the exercise.

3. Both partners take a few moments to reflect and discuss their experiences.

DAY SIXTEEN: PASSION/FITTING

THIS EXERCISE IS A DEMONSTRATION of a very basic form of transmission, an unevoked "state entity" being shared between two humans.

Sharing the Flow

1. Person B guides Person A through the process of selecting a powerful resource experience and developing an energy flow, as if beginning the simple evocation of a "Basic Positive Resource Entity." The energy flow remains in A's body, however. A keeps the content of the experience, the memory or initiating thought, private.
2. While partners sit facing each other, Person A teaches that particular energy flow to Person B by explaining where the feeling starts, what kind of feeling it is, where it moves or spreads to, how it cycles, what color(s) might be associated with the feeling, and so on.
3. Person B moves to sit beside A. Person A guides B into the energy flow again.
4. Person B and A switch seats (but not roles). Sitting where A was originally sitting at the beginning of the exercise, B is guided into the energy flow again.
5. Partners switch roles and repeat the exercise.
6. Both partners take a few moments to reflect and discuss their experiences.

DAY SEVENTEEN: PASSION/TRANCE

THIS EXERCISE BUILDS ON THE TRANSMISSION PRACTICE offered in "Sharing the Flow" (Day Sixteen). More complexity is added to the exercise, giving practical experience in the way that states, trances, and entities change with time. Neuroplasticity is also encouraged by this exercise.

Flow Trance

1. Partners sit facing each other. Person A demonstrates an energy flow for B to learn, as done in step 2 of the "Sharing the Flow" exercise.
2. When each partner has established a powerful energy flow, as taught by A, he or she informs the other partner. Continue on when both partners have announced their states.
3. Partners remain silent, seated comfortably, and in full view of each other, with eyes open. In this position, each begins to modify his or her own energy flow, exploring different sensory arrangements and submodalities to increase the effect of the flow and create a unique and powerful altered state. They continue for about ten minutes.
4. Partners then switch roles and repeat the experiment.
5. Both partners take a few moments to reflect and discuss their experiences.

DAY EIGHTEEN: PASSION/MAKING

THIS EXERCISE IS PERFORMED BY EACH PERSON INDIVIDUALLY.

Passion Entity

1. Define a circle around yourself and sit or stand in the exact center. Inhale and expand your attention to fill the circle. Exhale and contract your attention to a single point in the center of your chest. Repeat at least three times.
2. Take notice of six points, placed equal distances apart, along the circumference of the circle.
3. Recall the experience of performing the Day Thirteen exercise, "Increasing Passion." Think about what you saw as you practiced, what you heard, what you felt, and whether there were any notable tastes or smells. Whatever perceptual representations you make of this memory—whether they are images, sounds, voices, feelings, tastes, or smells—take a deep breath and project those representations into a sphere on one of the points on the circle. Take another deep breath and project the exhalation into the sphere.
4. Recall the experience of performing the Day Fourteen exercise, "Shifting Auras," and then project whatever perceptual representations you make of this memory into a sphere on one of the points on the circle. Take another deep breath and project the breath into the sphere.
5. Recall the experience of performing the Day Fifteen exercise, "The Story of Passion," and then project whatever perceptual representations

you make of this memory into a sphere on one of the points on the circle. Take another deep breath and project the breath into the sphere.

6. Recall the experience of performing the Day Sixteen exercise, "Sharing the Flow," and then project whatever perceptual representations you make of this memory into a sphere on one of the points on the circle. Take another deep breath and project the breath into the sphere.

7. Recall the experience of performing the Day Seventeen exercise, "Flow Trance," and then project whatever perceptual representations you make of this memory into a sphere on one of the points on the circle. Take another deep breath and project the breath into the sphere.

8. Take note of what you are doing now, the Day Eighteen exercise, "Passion Entity," and then project whatever perceptual representations you make of this experience into a sphere on one of the points on the circle. Take another deep breath and project the breath into the sphere.

9. Take a step backward, leaving the center of the circle empty.

10. Take a deep breath and direct your exhalation into the center of the circle. As you do so, allow the six spheres to draw inward, combining into a single shape in the center of the circle. Allow that shape to take whatever form seems natural to it. Continue to breathe deeply and project your breath into the shape.

11. In your thoughts, communicate with the entity. Find out if there is a special name or symbol that it would like to use. Find out if it knows what you have learned about passion from these exercises. Find out what else it can teach you, right now or later, about passion.

12. Have it explain, or decide along with the entity, how to quickly and easily resummon the entity at a later date. That might involve recalling a particular sensory element, saying a particular word or name, or following a method of any kind. Take note of this information so that you can use it later.

13. When you are finished, take a deep breath and draw the entity, any remaining spheres, and the circle back into yourself.

14. Repeat the expansion/contraction breathing as in step 1.

15. Take a few moments to reflect on what you have experienced.

DAY NINETEEN: FITTING/FITTING

BRAIN RESEARCHERS TALK ABOUT CELLS called mirror neurons, which are important in how we learn and transmit behavior. Mirror neurons were first identified in monkeys. An area of the brain became active when a monkey was observing and imitating the behavior, particularly the mouth movements, of other monkeys. It was just a short hop of research from monkeys to their primate cousins, the humans, who turned out also to have mirror neurons. Apparently, when one human observes the behavior of another, the mirror neurons go to work, creating a model of the behavior and then applying it to their own actions. Mirror neurons allow you to walk a mile in someone else's shoes, feel their pain or joy, and to empathize, sympathize, and develop rapport.

A Fitting Pair

1. Each partner, individually, accesses a positive resource state, developing an energy flow as in previous exercises.
2. While breathing deeply and evenly, each partner brings his or her flow to a strong, powerful level. When that level has been reached, each will let the feeling of the flow find expression as a movement or gesture, answering the question, "If this feeling were a movement, what would it be?"
3. Each partner takes time to learn the other person's movement or gesture. Partners demonstrate their movements for each other as often as is necessary to teach them.
4. Then, facing each other, each partner returns to his or her own movement, repeating it over and over, while keeping eyes open and observing the other partner.

5. As each partner watches the other, he or she begins to incorporate elements of the other's movement into his or her own. They continue incorporating each other's movements until a "partner movement" has been developed—a compromise or aggregate movement that both partners practice identically.
6. Partners practice the "partner movement" together for another minute.
7. Both partners take a few moments to reflect and discuss their experiences.

A Fitting Group

1. A partner pair that has accomplished the first exercise, "A Fitting Pair," meets with another partner pair. Each pair teaches its partner movement to the other pair, so that both pairs can do both movements.
2. Partners then revert to their own partner movement, repeating it while observing the other partner pair, who repeat their own partner movement. Gradually, each pair integrates elements from the other pair's partner movement until a "foursome movement" is developed.
3. Both pairs continue to practice the foursome movement together for at least another minute.
4. The entire group then convenes, and the foursomes each demonstrate their movements for the rest of the group, so that everyone can learn all the foursome movements.
5. Foursomes then revert to their own foursome movement, repeating it while observing the other foursomes. Gradually, each person integrates elements from the other foursomes until a "group movement" is developed.
6. The entire group continues to practice the group movement for at least another minute.
7. Participants take a few moments to reflect and discuss their experiences.

DAY TWENTY: FITTING/ATTENTION

THE MODELING ACTIVITY OF MIRROR NEURONS may be extended over a wide range of dissociated experiences. Indeed, Atem would suggest that mirror neurons are activated not only when observing humans, but also when observing or experiencing the behavior of any kind of entity that has a whole mind.

This exercise enhances communication, neuroplasticity, transmission, understanding, and opening.

Fitting to the World

Person A guides Person B through the following experience:

1. Sit comfortably with your eyes open and extend your attention to include an area greater than the room you are in. If possible, extend it to include the geographical location around you—that is, the neighborhood, the town, the city, the valley, the mountain, the island, or whatever best describes your location. You may use the Day Three "Expansion and Contraction" breathing exercises for this purpose.

2. Listen attentively to everything around you. Listen in three dimensions, so that you become aware of sounds in different locations around you, above you, or below you. Listen to the sounds that are close and the sounds that form the auditory background—wind, distant cars, rain, or whatever there might be.

3. As you continue to listen, look at everything that is within your sight. Notice color, movement or stillness, brightness, contrast, and so forth. Notice what is close, what is farther away. Visualize what cannot be immediately seen—whatever is behind you, whatever might be associ-

ated with the more distant sounds that you hear, whatever you might already know about the surrounding location.

4. As you continue to listen and to look, extend your sense of feeling to whatever is immediately in your presence. How does it feel to sit where you are sitting? How do your clothes feel? How does the air feel on any exposed skin? Then imagine the feeling of those things that you can hear, see, or visualize. Will the shiny floor feel smooth, rough, hard, soft, wet, dry, or whatever? How does the distant wind feel on skin? What does the upholstery in one of those distant cars feel like? Continue with a large number of kinesthetic details about things that are not immediately in contact with you, but that can be heard or seen.

5. Stay and experience in this way, with all senses involved, for a few minutes, then draw your attention back in to your body.

6. Partners then switch roles and repeat the exercise.

7. Both partners take a few moments to reflect and discuss their experiences.

DAY TWENTY-ONE: FITTING/LANGUAGE

ANY WAY THAT WE CREATE OR REPRESENT A MODEL of consciousness will have the ability to access the powerful learning associated with mirror neurons. Words will ultimately lead to the same ends as images, tunes, movement, etc.

Sharing Words

1. Partners create a "partner movement" as done in the exercise "A Fitting Pair" (Day Nineteen).
2. Partners then sit side by side, facing the same direction. Using peripheral vision as much as possible, partners observe each other.
3. Partners match each other's posture, breathing, and movements as much as possible. If one partner scratches his or her head, then the other scratches his or her own head in the same way. If one partner coughs, then the other coughs, too. And so on. Both partners continue to mirror each other through the rest of the exercise.
4. Person A describes his or her present experience in whatever way he or she can, mentioning at least two things in each sense and making sure to include both internal and external consciousness. For instance, "I feel comfortable sitting here and feel these soft cushions. And I keep saying to myself that there's more to this exercise and I notice the little sound I'm making with each breath. I see you in my peripheral vision

and also keep remembering what it looked like when we were making the partner movement."

5. Person B then takes a turn and similarly describes his or her experience.
6. Both partners take a few moments to reflect and discuss their experiences.

DAY TWENTY-TWO: FITTING/PASSION

HUMANS HAVE DEVELOPED MANY NATURAL WAYS TO ACTIVATE mirror neurons for purposes of fitting and learning. What mirroring behaviors do we engage in, either instinctively or culturally? How can these behaviors be used consciously?

Shared Feelings

1. With your partner, agree on three shared experiences that are acceptable to both of you. In each of these experiences, you will engage in behavior that naturally puts you into identical kinesthetic experiences. For instance, in a handshake both partners feel contact of skin on skin in the same place on the same hand. In making a toast, both partners feel the same feeling of a glass in the same hand as they make the same movement and say the same thing. These behaviors may or may not include physical contact. Some general examples are given below; fill in the specifics with your partner (i.e., what kind of handshake, what toast):
    *   Handshake
    *   Toast
    *   High five
    *   Shoulder clasping
    *   Salute
    *   Waving hello or goodbye
    *   Dance steps

- Partner yoga pose
- "Eskimo nose rubbing"
- Kissing (if acceptable in situation)
- Making love (if acceptable in situation)

2. Perform each behavior first at regular speed, then in slow motion—as slow as you can make it. As you perform the behavior, be aware of matching your partner's physiology as much as possible and making sure that you are moving or touching your partner with exactly the same motion or touch that he or she is using. For example, if your palm is touching his or hers in a handshake, make sure that exactly the same area and amount of your palm is involved as is your partner's.

3. After completing this process for three behaviors, switch positions with your partner so that you are each sitting or standing exactly where the other was when you performed step 2.

4. Repeat the three movements from the new positions, first at regular speed, then in slow motion, matching experience as closely as possible.

5. Take a few moments to reflect and discuss your experiences.

DAY TWENTY-THREE: FITTING/TRANCE

FOR HUMANS OR ENTITIES TO COMMUNICATE, words may or may not be necessary. States and a great deal of implied information can be conveyed silently.

Silent Induction #1

1. Partners sit side by side. Person A observes Person B using peripheral vision.
2. Person A matches B's rate of breathing, posture, movements, and facial expression.
3. When A feels that he or she is fitting comfortably with B, Person A then begins to deepen his or her breathing and to recall a personal experience of deep relaxation. A silently recalls the various sensory details of this experience—what could be seen, heard, and felt at the time.
4. A continues to check on B. If B appears to be following into the state of relaxation, A continues to deepen that experience. If after several minutes B has not yet changed state (noticed by such criteria as changes in rate of breathing, posture, and facial expression), A returns to matching B's behavior for a few minutes, then resumes the relaxation, repeating the process until B follows into a trance.
5. After a few minutes experiencing the trance, A brings him- or herself back to baseline and allows B to follow.
6. Partners switch positions and repeat the exercise.
7. Both partners take a few moments to reflect and discuss their experiences.

Silent Induction #2

1. In a group setting, participants sit in a circle.
2. By a random method, half the participants are selected to be in group A and half in group B. This method might involve pulling slips of paper marked A and B from a hat, or the choice might be at the discretion of the group leader or facilitator. Each person announces his or her letter as the letters are chosen.
3. The A's develop a pleasant and enjoyable energy flow. Each A imagines a circle around him- or herself and expands the energy flow to fill the circle.
4. After a few minutes, each A changes the shape of his or her circle to expand and envelop one of the B participants. Each A does this, as much as possible, without looking directly at the B, but paying attention to whether or not the B looks directly at him or her.
5. After a few minutes of this, participants switch roles and repeat the experiment.
6. The entire group takes a few moments to reflect and discuss its experiences.

DAY TWENTY-FOUR: FITTING/MAKING

THIS EXERCISE IS PERFORMED BY EACH PERSON INDIVIDUALLY.

Fitting Entity

1. Define a circle around you and sit or stand in the exact center. Inhale and expand your attention to fill the circle. Exhale and contract your attention to a single point in the center of your chest. Repeat at least three times.

2. Take notice of six points, placed equal distances apart, along the circumference of the circle.

3. Recall the experience of performing the Day Nineteen exercises, "A Fitting Pair" and "A Fitting Group." Think about what you saw as you practiced, what you heard, what you felt, and whether there were any notable tastes or smells. Whatever perceptual representations you make of these memories—whether they are images, sounds, voices, feelings, tastes, or smells—take a deep breath and project those representations into a sphere on one of the points located on the circle. Take another deep breath and project the exhalation into the sphere.

4. Recall the experience of performing the Day Twenty exercise, "Fitting to the World," and then project whatever perceptual representations you make of this memory into a sphere on one of the points on the circle. Take another deep breath and project the breath into the sphere.

5. Recall the experience of performing the Day Twenty-one exercise, "Sharing Words," and then project whatever perceptual representations

you make of this memory into a sphere on one of the points on the circle. Take another deep breath and project the breath into the sphere.

6. Recall the experience of performing the Day Twenty-two exercise, "Shared Feelings," and then project whatever perceptual representations you make of this memory into a sphere on one of the points on the circle. Take another deep breath and project the breath into the sphere.

7. Recall the experience of performing the Day Twenty-three exercises, "Silent Induction #1" and "Silent Induction #2," and then project whatever perceptual representations you make of these memories into a sphere on one of the points on the circle. Take another deep breath and project the breath into the sphere.

8. Take note of what you are doing now, the Day Twenty-four exercise, "Fitting Entity," and then project whatever perceptual representations you make of this experience into a sphere on one of the points on the circle. Take another deep breath and project the breath into the sphere.

9. Take a step backward, leaving the center of the circle empty.

10. Take a deep breath and direct your exhalation into the center of the circle. As you do so, allow the six spheres to draw inward, combining into a single shape in the center of the circle. Allow that shape to take whatever form seems natural to it. Continue to breathe deeply and project your breath into the shape.

11. In your thoughts, communicate with the entity. Find out if there is a special name or symbol that it would like to use. Find out if it knows what you have learned about fitting from these exercises. Find out what else it can teach you, right now or later, about fitting.

12. Have it explain, or decide along with the entity, how to quickly and easily resummon the entity at a later date. That might involve recalling a particular sensory element, saying a particular word or name, or following a method of any kind. Take note of this information so that you can use it later.

13. When you are finished, take a deep breath and draw the entity, any remaining spheres, and the circle back into yourself.

14. Repeat the expansion/contraction breathing as in step 1.

15. Take a few moments to reflect on what you have experienced.

DAY TWENTY-FIVE: TRANCE/TRANCE

WORKING FROM OUR DEFINITION OF A TRANCE as "a state of consciousness different than the one that preceded it," we can understand that we all have many, many different kinds of trances to work with. Being able to switch from one trance to another at will is a skill that encourages neuroplasticity, transformation, understanding, balance, and opening.

Trance Regression

1. Person A guides Person B to recall some method of consciousness alteration that he or she enjoyed as a small child. Most people have numerous examples, including spinning around, rolling down hills, daydreaming, staring at something, repeating words rhythmically or singing, hyperventilation or holding the breath, or conversing with an imaginary friend. B is guided through the senses and submodalities to access the altered state.

2. If it is possible and safe, B can actually perform the recalled method of trance induction.

3. B teaches the trance to A, either by explaining the submodalities involved or by demonstrating the actual method (spinning, chanting, breathing, or whatever).

4. Partners switch roles and repeat the exercise.

5. Both partners take a few moments to reflect and discuss their experiences.

Trance Now

1. Person A guides Person B to think of some method of consciousness alteration that he or she currently enjoys. Again, most people have numerous examples. These might include self-hypnosis, meditation, ritual work, yoga, taking a hot bath, listening to a favorite song, exercising, visiting a special place, or daydreaming. B is guided through the senses and submodalities to access an altered state.
2. If it is possible and safe, B can actually perform the method of trance induction.
3. B teaches the trance to A, either by explaining the submodalities involved or by demonstrating the actual method.
4. Partners switch roles and repeat the exercise.
5. Both partners take a few moments to reflect and discuss their experiences.

Trance to Come

1. Person A guides Person B to think of some variety of consciousness alteration he or she would like to experience in the future. Again, this can be of almost any sort—a very relaxing experience, a new form of meditation, a psychoactive substance, or a form of hypnosis; attending a particular concert; engaging in a ritual or ceremony; or whatever. B is guided to think about what that might or will look like, sound like, feel like, taste like, and smell like, with as much submodality information as possible.
2. If it is possible and safe, B can actually perform the imagined method of trance induction.
3. B teaches the trance to A, either by explaining the submodalities involved or by demonstrating the actual method.
4. Partners switch roles and repeat the exercise.
5. Both partners take a few moments to reflect and discuss their experience.

DAY TWENTY-SIX:
TRANCE/ATTENTION

A TRANCE, IN PART, DEFINES HOW AND WHERE we put our attention. In some trances we may be motivated to behave in ways that we think of as useful, powerful, or evolutionary; in other trances we may find it difficult to transcend our state. This exercise is continued practice in shifting states at will.

Urge Mapping

1. Person A asks Person B questions to map the submodalities for thoughts and representations of the following:

    a. A neutral behavior (talking on the phone, watching TV, eating a snack, or something else that recurs sporadically, not necessarily at regular times).

    b. The urge to transcendence. Where and when do you have the urge to alter consciousness in a significant way? This could include the impetus to meditate, perform a ritual, climb a mountain, practice yoga, fast, have an orgasm, consume an entheogenic substance, appreciate the beauty of a forest, or whatever you consider transcendence. Pay attention to the urge that occurs just prior to the activity, not necessarily the activity itself.

    c. The urge to ritual. For this purpose, a ritual is any complex activity that is repeated for a beneficial effect. It could be a religious or ceremonial ritual or a ritual such as showering, brushing teeth, or making breakfast. The important part is that the behavior is something that is replicated, with motivation, on a regular basis. Remember to pay attention to the urge that occurs just prior to the activity.

    d. Another practice that B would like to have the urge to explore on a daily basis, but does not yet engage in.

2. In mapping these urges, note the following:

    a. What senses are involved? What are the submodalities of those senses (i.e., location, size, movement, stillness, volume, intensity, and so on).

    b. Does Person B include him- or herself in the representation, as if seeing, hearing, or feeling it from another person's point of view? Or is it created from his or her own point of view?

3. Person A notes what is significantly different between the representation of the neutral behavior and the urges to ritual and to transcendence. A selects what appears to be the most significant of these differences (such as sense, location, or size) and guides B through the process of applying these submodalities to the behavior that B would like to be motivated to practice.

4. Partners switch roles and repeat the exercise.

5. Both partners take a few moments to reflect and discuss their experiences.

DAY TWENTY-SEVEN: TRANCE/LANGUAGE

THIS EXERCISE MAKES USE OF A CLASSIC hypnotic phenomenon, arm catalepsy, to calibrate the effects of a spoken induction of relaxation.

Guided Trance

1. Using language with as little specific content as possible, Person A guides Person B to access a state of relaxation. For instance, this guidance can make use of a memory of a time when B was very relaxed, as opposed to offering a specific scenario; that is, instead of saying, "You are sitting at the beach, feeling very relaxed," A might say "Remember a time and place when you were very relaxed." Let B silently fill in the details.
2. Person A lightly takes hold of B's wrist and gently lifts B's arm up while continuing to talk. A instructs B to "just let the arm hang there in the air, just like that." (See fig. C on page 71.) If B's attention is properly directed toward the relaxing experience, the arm will stay in whatever position it is left.
3. A instructs B to "allow your unconscious mind to lower the arm only as fast as you become relaxed, and allow it to rise with unconscious movements if you should become less relaxed." A illustrates this direction by gently pushing down and up to move B's arm as the instructions are spoken.

4. Person A continues to guide B through the experience, continuing to be as vague as possible. For instance, A might ask B to note the temperature of the air (as opposed to "the cool breeze"), the colors that can be seen, the sounds that can be heard, or the feelings that can be felt. A can go into detail using submodality distinctions but can continue to avoid any specific content.

5. A notes what kinds of things help B become more relaxed and repeats or expands on those things until B's arm has lowered completely or until about five minutes have passed. For instance, if visual experiences make B's arm rise and auditory experiences make B's arm lower, A uses less and less visual language and more of the auditory submodalities that add to B's relaxation.

6. Partners switch roles and repeat the exercise.

7. Both partners take a few moments to reflect and discuss their experiences.

DAY TWENTY-EIGHT: TRANCE/PASSION

ONCE AGAIN, BREATHING CAN BE USED as a very direct method to alter consciousness. If each state can be thought of as associated with a particular entity, then different methods or habits of breathing can be used to access this variety of entities. This exercise helps to develop powers of communication, neuroplasticity, transformation, beauty, and opening.

Ecstatic Breathing

1. Breathe through your mouth, slowly and evenly, for about one minute.
2. Breathe by drawing the air into the bottommost part of your lungs, deep into your belly. Start with a slow, even pace, then gradually increase the rate until, finally, you are panting, but still filling and emptying the deepest part of your lungs.
3. Continue to pant for half a minute, then take a deep, full breath, filling your lungs from top to bottom. Hold the breath for ten seconds, then release and breathe slowly and deeply a few times. Return to panting and repeat this cycle until you have deepened your trance state.

Orgasmic Recall

1. After completing the "Ecstatic Breathing" exercise, allow your breathing to find its own rhythm as you perform the following steps.
2. Recall the feeling just prior to your most recent orgasm. Remember what you saw and heard at the time. Where in your body does the feeling begin? Where does it move to? How exactly does it build? How much of your body does the feeling move through as it approaches the moment of orgasm?
3. Assign a color or colors to the feeling, answering the question, "If this feeling had a color, what would it be?"
4. Hold out a hand, palm up, and then externalize the colored shape, imagining or allowing it to move out of your body and condense into a form that will fit on your palm.
5. Touch that hand to different parts of your body and notice how it feels.
6. If possible and appropriate, touch someone else with that hand.
7. Draw the colored shape back into your body and allow it to return to its proper location and size.
8. Take a few moments to reflect on your experience.

DAY TWENTY-NINE: TRANCE/FITTING

THIS EXERCISE IS DECEPTIVELY SIMPLE and yet embodies an interesting, broad range of trance phenomena. Nothing is *supposed* to happen, but several things may.

Watch the Hand Move

1. Partners sit opposite each other, with eyes open.
2. They begin by matching each other's posture, breathing, and facial expressions.
3. Both rest their left hands and forearms on their upper leg, in full view of each other.
4. In soft, calm voices each begins to instruct the other to "watch the hand move."
5. Speaking simultaneously, partners continue to repeat the instruction, over and over, while also following the direction and watching their partner's left hand.
6. Partners continue to watch and speak for at least ten minutes.
7. Both partners take a few moments to reflect and discuss their experiences.

DAY THIRTY: TRANCE/MAKING

THIS EXERCISE IS PERFORMED BY EACH PERSON INDIVIDUALLY.

Trance Entity

1. Define a circle around you and sit or stand in the exact center. Inhale and expand your attention to fill the circle. Exhale and contract your attention to a single point in the center of your chest. Repeat at least three times.
2. Take notice of six points, placed equal distances apart, along the circumference of the circle.
3. Recall the experience of performing the Day Twenty-five exercises, "Trance Regression," "Trance Now," and "Trance to Come." Think about what you saw as you practiced, what you heard, what you felt, and whether there were any notable tastes or smells. Whatever perceptual representations you make of these memories—whether they are images, sounds, voices, feelings, tastes, or smells—take a deep breath and project those representations into a sphere on one of the points on the circle. Take another deep breath and project the exhalation into the sphere.
4. Recall the experience of performing the Day Twenty-six exercise, "Urge Mapping," and then project whatever perceptual representations you make of this memory into a sphere on one of the points on the circle. Take another deep breath and project the breath into the sphere.
5. Recall the experience of performing the Day Twenty-Seven exercise, "Guided Trance," and then project whatever perceptual representations

you make of this memory into a sphere on one of the points on the circle. Take another deep breath and project the breath into the sphere.

6. Recall the experience of performing the Day Twenty-eight exercises, "Ecstatic Breathing" and "Orgasmic Recall," and then project whatever perceptual representations you make of these memories into a sphere on one of the points on the circle. Take another deep breath and project the breath into the sphere.

7. Recall the experience of performing the Day Twenty-nine exercise, "Watch the Hand Move," and then project whatever perceptual representations you make of this memory into a sphere on one of the points on the circle. Take another deep breath and project the breath into the sphere.

8. Take note of what you are doing now, the Day Thirty exercise, "Trance Entity," and then project whatever perceptual representations you make of this experience into a sphere on one of the points on the circle. Take another deep breath and project the breath into the sphere.

9. Take a step backward, leaving the center of the circle empty.

10. Take a deep breath and direct your exhalation into the center of the circle. As you do so, allow the six spheres to draw inward, combining into a single shape in the center of the circle. Allow that shape to take whatever form seems natural to it. Continue to breathe deeply and project your breath into the shape.

11. In your thoughts, communicate with the entity. Find out if there is a special name or symbol that it would like to use. Find out if it knows what you have learned about trance from these exercises. Find out what else it can teach you, right now or later, about trance.

12. Have it explain, or decide along with the entity, how to quickly and easily resummon the entity at a later date. That might involve recalling a particular sensory element, saying a particular word or name, or following a method of any kind. Take note of this information so that you can use it later.

13. When you are finished, take a deep breath and draw the entity, any remaining spheres, and the circle back into yourself.

14. Repeat the expansion/contraction breathing as in step 1.

15. Take a few moments to reflect on what you have experienced.

DAY THIRTY-ONE: MAKING/ATTENTION

"Ideomotor testing" makes use of the human body's ability to communicate on an unconscious level. Every thought, every concept, every state of consciousness will have its effects on the muscles, circulatory system, respiratory system, and organs. This principle can be tested using biofeedback devices ranging from simple heart-rate monitors to galvanic skin-response monitors to brain-activity monitors of every sort. The principle can also be tested without any special equipment by noticing subtle movement and changes in the body.

Making is fulfilled when testing is complete.

Basic Energy Testing

1. Person A stands with one arm outstretched directly to one side, at the level of the shoulder—relaxed, but maintaining the position. Person B places one hand on A's opposite shoulder and then rests two fingers lightly just above the wrist of A's outstretched hand. (See fig. D.)

Figure D

2. B first calibrates, determining how strong A's outstretched arm is in that position by exerting a small amount of pressure with his or her two fingers on A's arm. Note that this action is not a test of strength, nor is it a contest; it is a means of simply testing how much force is necessary to move the arm.

3. A then makes a statement that is obviously true—for instance "My name is" and his or her name. B then tests the arm.
4. A then makes a statement that is obviously false—for instance, "My name is (someone else's name)." B then tests the arm.
5. Partners then switch roles and repeat the exercise.
6. Both partners take a few moments to reflect and discuss their experiences.

Balance Testing

1. This exercise is a solo means of testing. First stand in a stable and balanced position, with your feet about hip's width apart, toes facing forward.
2. Make a statement that is obviously true and notice how your balance is affected; notice whether you are leaning slightly forward or slightly back. The response motions may be very subtle and you may be required to wait a few seconds for them or repeat the statement until the response movements become noticeable.
3. Make a statement that is obviously false and notice how your balance is affected.
4. Take a few moments to reflect on what you have experienced.

Testing Your Life

1. Using either method of testing, select some of your own behaviors, habits, likes and dislikes, and test them.
2. Phrase each test as a statement rather than a question—for example, "Spinach is good for me," "I watch too much TV," "I will be happy if I ask so-and-so for a date."
3. Follow up each test with more specific statements, where appropriate—for example, "I eat enough spinach," "I will be healthiest if I eat twice as much spinach," "I will feel best if I ask so-and-so for a date by telephone on Friday evening."
4. Take a few moments to reflect on what you have experienced.

DAY THIRTY-TWO:
MAKING/LANGUAGE

TO MAKE SOMETHING IN ANY FIELD OF ENDEAVOR, it is very helpful to clearly and fully imagine a large part of it in advance. For either internal or external parts of consciousness to understand what routes or mechanisms may deliver the desired outcome, there must be enough detail to suggest the entire process, if only on an unconscious level. This act of imagination often begins on the level of expressed language and then fills in details in multiple submodalities in every sense.

Outcomes, as stated, can be imagined in any field of endeavor, including the desired result of a business transaction, the creation of an oil painting, the evolution of an interpersonal relationship, or the creation of a paradigm-shifting memetic entity.

Stating Your Outcome

1. State your outcome in a single sentence, making it as concise as possible.
2. Check that the outcome is stated as a positive, and make the statement descriptive rather than a command or a wish. For instance, "I want a million dollars" or "Give me the Mona Lisa" are a wish and a command, respectively. "I will not get angry" is a negative statement. Better suggestions include "I will hold a check in my hand for one million dollars," "The *Mona Lisa* will hang on this wall," and "I can feel relaxed and comfortable in every situation."

3. Use ideomotor testing of some sort to verify that this outcome is (a) possible and (b) good for you. If not, begin again. If so, continue with the next exercise.

Imagining Your Outcome

1. Begin with the statement you developed in the previous exercise. Add in details about how the outcome will look, how it will feel, how it will sound as you experience what the statement describes. For instance, holding a check for a million dollars in your hand will have certain characteristics that can be seen (the numbers written on the check, for instance), heard (the rustle or crinkling of paper), and felt (the feel of paper in your hand).

2. Then think about how you will feel, emotionally or internally, once this has happened. If you receive a check for a million dollars, you might feel happy, relieved, exultant, determined to use it in a particular way, or whatever.

3. Repeat steps 1 and 2, but if you first imagined the sensory details from your own point of view—that is, seeing, hearing, feeling as if with your own eyes, ears, and body—then imagine the details as if from the sensory equipment of an observer, seeing yourself in the image, hearing your own voice, if that's a part of it, and so on. If you first imagined the sensory details from the point of view of an observer, then imagine it from your point of view.

4. Use ideomotor testing of some sort to verify that this outcome is (a) possible and (b) good for you. If not, begin again. If so, continue to the Day Thirty-three exercises.

5. Take a few moments to reflect on what you have experienced.

DAY THIRTY-THREE: MAKING/PASSION

PASSION IS USEFUL IN MAKING for its ability to ensure purity of outcome. Attention is carried by and empowered by passion. The more that your outcome is aligned with congruence and power, the more likely you are to attain it. Passion is built by the accumulating energy, aligning sensory submodalities, and sometimes by isolating the pure elements of a particular state, idea, concept, or experience. The process of isolating elements of an experience could be used as a definition of evocation.

Aligning Imagination with Outcome

1. Select three experiences: one that represents something you have not wanted and have never tried to get; one that represents something you tried to get but didn't; and one that represents something you really, really wanted and were powerfully motivated to get, and you got it. The latter could be something as life changing as a new relationship or a new career, or it could relate to material goods—anything from a new house to a chocolate bar.
2. Notice how you create each of these three representations—in what senses you imagine them, the size of the imagining, and so on, a process similar to that used in Day Thirteen's "Increasing Passion" exercise. The goal is to identify what submodalities are uniquely and closely associated with really, really wanting something and being powerfully motivated to successfully achieve it.
3. Once you have identified the submodalities of success, return your attention to your imagined outcome from the Day Thirty-two exercises. Apply the submodalities to your imagining of the outcome. If you

identified that the things you really want and are powerfully motivated to get are represented as very large images with bright colors and a glow, then apply those qualities to your imagined outcome. If you discovered that your success formula involved melodious sounds around your head, then apply those submodalities to your imagined outcome, and so on, adapting the imagined outcome to whatever your preferred way of representing an experience of success might be.

4. Notice if you feel or behave differently toward your imagined outcome.
5. Take a few moments to reflect on what you have experienced.

Creating and Empowering a State Entity

1. Contemplate your aligned outcome experience from the previous exercise. Notice any feelings associated with it.
2. Create an internal experience in which you see/hear yourself having already achieved this particular outcome. Notice any feelings associated with this internal experience.
3. Step into that experience, so you that can directly experience what it feels like to have achieved this particular outcome.
4. Use the feelings in your body to evoke an entity, as in the "Basic Positive Resource Entity" exercise in the "Simple Evocations" section. This type of entity is called a *State Entity*.
5. Breathe deeply and fully and charge the entity by exhaling into it six to eight times.
6. Notice how the entity has changed or transformed, then draw it, along with all other imaginings from this exercise, back into your body.
7. Take a few moments to reflect on what you have experienced.

DAY THIRTY-FOUR: MAKING/FITTING

ALL COMMUNICATION DEPENDS ON FITTING. We can communicate with each other when we use a common language, when we are, at least to some extent, comfortable with each other, and when our intent and attention is somewhat aligned. If you are in an interaction with another human or an entity that has a different idea of the purpose of the communication, the exchange will likely end quickly, or you will waste time without reaching a mutually useful outcome. If, however, two participants in a discussion both desire the same outcome for the exchange, then the communication can move swiftly and easily toward a mutually useful outcome.

Fitting with Your State Entity

1. Evoke a state entity as in the Day Thirty-three exercise "Creating and Empowering a State Entity."
2. Empower the entity with deep breathing.
3. Choose one of the methods of ideomotor testing described in the Day Thirty-one exercises or another method you might know, such as using a pendulum or dowsing tool, finger signaling, or whatever works well for you and will provide yes/no responses.
4. Establish through questioning and ideomotor testing that the state entity is agreeable and will assist you in your efforts to make your outcome. Find out how much breath energy the entity requires to send your outcome to the parts of internal and external consciousness necessary for the outcome's completion. The number of breaths can be determined

by stating numbers sequentially and testing each: "One breath is the optimum number to empower my outcome." Test. "Two breaths are the optimum number." Test.

5. Next, establish internal verbal communication with the state entity, as in simple evocations. Talk with it. Learn the name or symbols of the state entity. Learn if the entity has any special requirements or tasks that you can perform to help it send your outcome to the parts of internal and external consciousness necessary for the outcome's completion.

6. Draw the entity, along with any other imaginings from this exercise, back into your body.

7. Take a few moments to reflect on what you have experienced.

DAY THIRTY-FIVE: MAKING/TRANCE

THE FOLLOWING EXERCISE IS A SIMPLE FORMULA for achieving a very wide range of outcomes. It is recommended that this exercise be practiced on a daily basis, using the same outcome, over an extended period of time. As internal and external consciousness begins to process the information, you can adjust, modify, and add to your imagined outcome; that is, as you start to understand what is involved in making your outcome happen, you can add these details into your imaginings. For instance, your outcome is to write a book on a specific subject. You work with the outcome of a finished book and a state entity that has been created from the feeling of the book having been finished. The information may come to you that to make this outcome, you'll need to work in a special, quiet place to get your writing done, so you add that special quiet place into your successive imaginings. Or you may realize that you need a certain amount of money to buy ink or paper for your printer. You can then add this detail into your imaginings—and so on until the entire process is revealed to you in detail.

Making an Outcome

1. Develop your outcome as in the previous exercises.
2. Create a state entity from the kinesthetic part of the outcome experience and fit with it as described in the Day Thirty-four "Fitting with Your State Entity" exercise.
3. Give the state entity an appropriate amount of breath energy, exhaling into it.
4. Imagine your outcome in detail and with submodalities aligned for success.

5. Give the imagining to the state entity, so that all the sensory details of the experience are absorbed by the entity.
6. Instruct the state entity to send the outcome, along with the breath energy, to the parts of internal and external consciousness that will be appropriate for making the outcome.
7. After the sensory experience and breath energy have been sent, thank the state entity for its cooperation and then reabsorb it into yourself.
8. Take a few moments to reflect on what you have experienced.
9. Repeat this exercise daily until your outcome is made.

DAY THIRTY-SIX: MAKING/MAKING

THIS EXERCISE IS PERFORMED BY EACH PERSON INDIVIDUALLY.

Making Entity

1. Define a circle around you and sit or stand in the exact center. Inhale and expand your attention to fill the circle. Exhale and contract your attention to a single point in the center of your chest. Repeat at least three times.

2. Take notice of six points, placed equal distances apart, along the circumference of the circle.

3. Recall the experience of performing the Day Thirty-one exercises, "Basic Energy Testing," "Balance Testing," and "Testing Your Life." Think about what you saw as you practiced, what you heard, what you felt, and whether there were any notable tastes or smells. Whatever perceptual representations you make of these memories—whether they are images, sounds, voices, feelings, tastes, or smells—take a deep breath and project those representations into a sphere on one of the points on the circle. Take another deep breath and project the exhalation into the sphere.

4. Recall the experience of performing the Day Thirty-two exercises, "Stating Your Outcome" and "Imagining Your Outcome," and then project whatever perceptual representations you make of these memories into a sphere on one of the points on the circumference. Take another deep breath and project the breath into the sphere.

5. Recall the experience of performing the Day Thirty-three exercises, "Aligning Imagination with Outcome" and "Creating and Empowering a State Entity," and then project whatever perceptual representations

you make of these memories into a sphere on one of the points on the circle. Take another deep breath and project the breath into the sphere.

6. Recall the experience of performing the Day Thirty-four exercise, "Fitting with Your State Entity," and then project whatever perceptual representations you make of this memory into a sphere on one of the points on the circle. Take another deep breath and project the breath into the sphere.

7. Recall the experience of performing the Day Thirty-five exercise, "Making an Outcome," and then project whatever perceptual representations you make of this memory into a sphere on one of the points on the circle. Take another deep breath and project the breath into the sphere.

8. Take note of what you are doing now, the Day Thirty-six exercise, "Making Entity," and then project whatever perceptual representations you make of this experience into a sphere on one of the points on the circle. Take another deep breath and project the breath into the sphere.

9. Take a step backward, leaving the center of the circle empty.

10. Take a deep breath and direct your exhalation into the center of the circle. As you do so, allow the six spheres to draw inward, combining into a single shape in the center of the circle. Allow that shape to take whatever form seems natural to it. Continue to breathe deeply and project your breath into the shape.

11. In your thoughts, communicate with the entity. Find out if there is a special name or symbol that it would like to use. Find out if it knows what you have learned about making from these exercises. Find out what else it can teach you, right now or later, about making.

12. Have it explain, or decide along with the entity, how to quickly and easily resummon the entity at a later date. That might involve recalling a particular sensory element, saying a particular word or name, or following a method of any kind. Take note of this information so that you can use it later.

13. When you are finished, take a deep breath and draw the entity, any remaining spheres, and the circle back into yourself.

14. Repeat the expansion/contraction breathing as in step 1.

15. Take a few moments to reflect on what you have experienced.

PART THREE
The Greater Evocation of Atem

INVOCATION OF SIX ELEMENTS

THIS EXERCISE IS A PREREQUISITE to activating this copy of *Meta-Magick: The Book of Atem*. At least one complete experience of the "Thirty-six Days of Atem" is necessary to perform the Invocation of Six Elements.

Find some time and space where you can be alone and uninterrupted for a little while. Turn off phones, computers, or any other possible distractions. This ritual can be practiced with eyes open or closed, whichever is easiest for you. You can also choose to move physically to face each direction, as necessary, or remain still, turning your attention to the different points.

1. **Imagine a circle** around you at a distance greater than arms' length. Choose six points that are spaced equidistant from each other on the circle.

2. Use the methods that the elemental entities have given you to resummon them. Evoke the **Attention** Entity, **Language** Entity, **Passion** Entity, **Fitting** Entity, **Trance** Entity, and **Making** Entity onto the six points on your circle.

3. **Imagine that each of the entities positioned around the circle is stretching out a tendril,** a long strand of itself, toward the center of the circle, where you are standing.

4. **Let the entities meet in the center.** Take a deep breath, and draw each of the entities fully into you, so that they all mingle together. Watch, listen, and feel as they mingle. Notice what shapes this process takes—what it looks like or sounds like or feels like. Notice if the combined entity changes colors, tones, or texture, or any other way it behaves as it fully joins together in the center of the circle.

5. **Pay particular attention to how this *feels*** inside and outside you. Notice where in your body the feeling begins, where it moves to, what

kind of feeling it is, whether it cycles or pulses, and anything else that you can notice about this feeling or feelings. Notice if there are any colors or sounds associated with the feeling.

6. Allow the feeling to build in you, take a deep breath, and then **express this feeling as a sound or a gesture** or both. Make careful note of this sound or gesture so that you can repeat it later, to resummon this experience. We will refer to this as your Six Elements Symbol.

7. In a loud, clear voice, **say, "Atem."**

8. Remain silent and still for at least a few minutes as you **take notice of whatever may result** from your actions. See, hear, and feel whatever it is that you see, hear, and feel now.

9. **Absorb** any leftover imaginings from this ritual back into yourself, including the circle itself.

EVOCATION OF ATEM: ACTIVATING YOUR BOOK

Book as Talisman

META-MAGICK: THE BOOK OF ATEM can function as a talisman. As Atem reminds us, any contact with this book or any of the ideas herein serves to empower Atem. Any amount of attention at all ensures his existence, and, of course, greater amounts of attention enable Atem to act in greater and more powerful ways.

You now have all the tools and components to evoke Atem into this book, if you choose to do so. This act can manifest the thought patterns and worldview of Atem in your consciousness and can serve as a quick and effective way for you to contact Atem at will. On the following pages, a simple and powerful exercise will guide you to create a sigil and draw it on the page. Space is provided for you to do this.

If you open this book and find sigils on the following pages, it means that this book has already been activated and is a unique talisman of a memetic entity. More sigils can be added, each increasing the flow of attention and information that is associated with the book. If there are presently no sigils in the book, you now have the opportunity to activate this copy.

Evocation of Atem

This exercise requires a writing instrument. Use one of your choice—pen, pencil, marker, crayon, or paintbrush. The sigil page can hold up to eight sigils, so use the space accordingly. When the sigil page is full, more sigils can be created inside the covers or in any place where the sigil can be drawn without crossing over into text or images. You will need to have practiced the Thirty-six Days of Atem and Invocation of Six Elements before attempting this exercise.

1. **Banish** with expansion/contraction breathing.
2. **Make the sound or gesture that is your six elements symbol.** Repeat this symbol as necessary, until the feeling associated with it is strong.
3. **Strengthen the feeling** even more by making it move through more and more of your body. Breathe deeply.
4. **Give the feeling a color.** As in simple evocations, apply a color or colors to the feeling, so that you can perceive a colored shape in your body, a map of where the feeling moves inside you.
5. **Externalize the colored shape.** Flip it around so that it faces you, and place it before you. Breathe deeply and exhale into the entity.
6. **Create a sigil** by drawing the shape of the entity into the book, on page 134. More detail is better, but a simple outline will work effectively. Continue breathing deeply and exhaling into the entity throughout.
7. **Apply the entity to the sigil.** Take the colored shape and, using your hands or just your mind, condense it down and place it on the sigil, so that the thought-form interpenetrates the drawn form.
8. In a loud, clear voice, **say "Atem."**
9. **Banish** again with expansion/contraction breathing.
10. **Hold the book in your hands** while you take a few moments to reflect on what you have experienced.

Sigil Page

PART FOUR
Creation of Memetic Entities

INTRODUCTION

THE GREATEST WORK THAT A HUMAN CAN ENGAGE IN is perfection of the self. Common wisdom suggests that we are best when we set our own being in order before imposing our will upon the world around us. On the level of ordinary, day-to-day activities, this makes a great deal of sense. Any works that we create will reflect our own psyche, for good or ill. A person with a disordered mind likely has a disordered desk. A person who hates and fears will create works and perform actions of hate and fear. A person who loves and meditates will likely create works of love and meditation.

The greatest work that a human can engage in is perfection of the self. But what are the boundaries of the self? In the wisdom of Atem, consciousness is not limited by the human body, and when we speak of our "self," we may be including many aspects of external consciousness as well as internal consciousness. With that in mind, when we address the idea of creating memetic entities, forms of consciousness that may have widespread and pervasive influence on the world around us, the creator is often something other than just the simple human internal consciousness. Indeed, by definition, a memetic entity depends on multiple human consciousnesses, or it would not be "memetic." As well, the process of entity creation as outlined by Atem involves the consciousness of various entities as well as that of humans.

A memetic entity usually participates in its own creation. It may begin as something simple in the internal or external consciousness of a single human, an entity formed from a simple evocation or similar approach. To achieve full stature as a memetic entity, it must then grow and evolve beyond the single human. This can happen by a variety of means. The entity can provide feedback to the human, who will then adjust and expand his or her ideas and actions. The entity can begin to include other humans or can access other entities for information or specific results. The entity can incorporate other entities in a variety of ways, some of them participating very much as an individual human might.

To be fully realized as a memetic entity, a mind must be whole, self-programming, able to transmit, able to reproduce, and must exhibit flexibility of behavior and adaptability to its environment.

A mind must be whole. What this means is that the entity must be or include a reflection of the universe at large. Just as the human mind builds a map or model within that represents a more or less complete world, the memetic entity must also be able to have some representation of the whole upon which to act.

A mind must be self-programming. The memetic entity must, at some point, be able to be free from the limits of a single human consciousness and to change itself and grow. This change and growth can be on the level of feedback given to the human creators or hosts, it may represent group consensus of participating humans, or it can be entirely independent of the human level of conscious awareness.

A memetic entity must be able to transmit. To survive beyond the awareness of a single human or group of humans, the entity must have assets that allow it to spread to more and more human and entity minds, as well as to media, architecture, consumer goods, or whatever else it tends to inhabit.

A memetic entity must be able to reproduce. A memetic entity will be capable of spawning other memetic entities, just as any other fully formed consciousness will. If a human or collection of humans can produce a memetic entity, then a memetic entity can produce other memetic entities. It may or may not choose to do so but nonetheless will have the ability, just as a healthy human has the ability to reproduce but may or may not choose to have children.

A memetic entity must exhibit flexibility of behavior and adaptability to its environment. An entity of any type that fails to adapt to changing circumstances will eventually cease to exist. When African loas met Roman Catholic religion, the loas were able to cloak themselves in the guises of the saints and thus survive in the New World. When the European worship of the fertility goddess Astarte met Christian religion, she incorporated herself into the holiday of Easter. This postulate is the essence of syncretism in religion and thought. It also describes how successful corporations adapt and vary their products based on changing demographics, economy, or other factors.

A memetic entity can exist anywhere in the noosphere and can manifest through any medium. The entity is the information and the self-organizing principle, and may be transmitted through books, visual art, video, film, architecture, corporate cultures, money, or anything else with the capability for storing or transmitting information. As the information spreads to more humans, the number and diversity of media will likely increase as the individual humans create their own expressions of the entity.

For the purposes of this text, Atem has selected several representative memetic entities to explore and reminds readers that the same principles will apply over a wide range of content and expression. The following descriptions and further elaboration are not necessarily intended to endorse any of these entities, but rather to use them to illustrate principles of memetic entity creation.

Money. Money is an extremely powerful, entrenched, and adaptable entity. Traditionally it has been transmitted through the use of talismans empowered by the entity in ritual circumstances. That money has a value is an idea only. There is nothing inherently valuable in the paper it is printed on, the metal that coins are stamped from, or the digits that accumulate electronically in bank accounts. Money may have had value at one time, as useful or inherently valuable things were traded; then markers, coins, and paper were used to represent the useful or valuable things. Then the markers were given value in and of themselves, and, most recently, numbers representing relative quantities of value are traded, without even physical markers. The action and scope of money in the world, transmitted with the aid of nearly every human on the planet, is beyond comprehension by any single human mind.

Rock and roll. Music that was indistinguishable from rock and roll existed for decades before the memetic entity came to life and spread the rhythms and sounds. Elements of rhythm and blues, boogie woogie, African shuffles and sand music, and Celtic melodies had been combined for years. It was only when disc jockey Alan Fried began to play the music over the radio and coined the term *rock and roll* that the entity was able to transmit itself. The term itself began as *rocking,* a reference among black musicians to spiritual experiences, then picked up an innuendo referring to the sex act, then referred to rhythm and dancing in general. The memetic entity rock and roll has retained that entire range of meaning, and continues to be spread through easily recognized rhythms and chord structures and a culture of human participants. In essence, the entity is spread by experience and even possession.

Legba. Legba is a loa, an entity in both African and New World religions (such as Voodoo), that holds a place similar to Atem. Legba stands at a symbolic crossroads and is a sort of gatekeeper, allowing or denying communication between humans and the spirit realm. Like rock and roll, Legba and most other loas are associated with easily recognized rhythms. Loas in general began as humans back in the distant past, and distinguished themselves in ways that made them legends. As their legends grew and began to incorporate the stories of other similarly inclined humans, they achieved the status of loas. Legba is spread through participation in any Voodoo ritual; he is the loa that is always called first, to open the way for the other entities. Again, like rock and roll, Legba is spread through experience and possession. Legba serves as an example of a memetic entity taking the form of a mythological god or goddess and as an example of how ancestors and historical figures can rise to the level of memetic entity.

Aikido. Aikido is a modern Japanese martial art that transmits a wealth of information about human behavior and spirituality via a simple system of mostly nonverbal practice and teaching. The set of martial techniques used in Aikido existed in very similar form in other fighting systems, including Daito Ryu jujitsu and in Japanese sword fighting. When Morihei Ueshiba aligned these techniques under a single name and emphasized the spiritual and nonviolent components, the memetic entity was born. Ueshiba adapted existing martial arts training into a teaching method that involved demonstration, imitation, and a paradigm whereby students would help and cooperate with each other. The teaching method allowed for transmission of Aikido, and its often unspoken principles, to every part of the world.

Democracy. Democracy is a unique form of group entity that has successfully spread very quickly throughout the world. The word literally means rule by *demos,* a group of humans that makes political decisions in a collective manner. In our modern usage of the term, we refer to a representative system of government in which citizens vote for government officials and sometimes directly for specific policies. The entity began by manifesting in philosophical documents and in ancient variants of the political system. It transmitted itself through further philosophical and political writings and by conquest, revolution, and other means. The success of the entity can be measured by the number of nations who have adopted a democratic system and universal suffrage (that is, entitlement to vote for all adult citizens, regardless of race or sex). There were no such nations in 1900; presently there are 120: 62 percent of all nations on Earth. Some of these nations' governments have evolved or mutated beyond the original, strict definitions of democracy, but nonetheless use the name and perpetuate the entity in numerous ways.

The Internet. In a 1997 speech, Tim Berners-Lee, who is generally credited as one of the principal inventors of the World Wide Web, described the Internet by saying, "We are forming cells within a global brain, and we are excited that we might start to think collectively. What becomes of us still hangs crucially on how we think individually." This is, of course, a perfect description of the interaction between humans and a memetic entity. As with the other entities that have just been described, the Internet existed in bits and pieces prior to the emergence of the memetic entity. Computer networks including ARPANET, NSFNet, and elements of the United States Department of Defense computer system were among the pieces that, by the late 1990s, had been collectively integrated into the global network we now know as the Internet. The Internet has evolved to the point where its growth, evolution, and response are well beyond the comprehension of any single human mind.

Corporations. To Atem's understanding, corporations are one of the most obvious forms of memetic entity. The word itself derives from the Latin *corpus,* meaning a "group of people." The *Oxford English Dictionary* defines *corporation* as "a group of people authorized to act as an individual." Indeed, the term *legal entity* is frequently applied to the idea of a corporation. The entity is empowered to perform a specific set of actions and very quickly develops its own cultural standards and values based on presuppositions that are included in the corporation's mission statement, articles of incorporation, and by-laws. All corporations exist through an interaction with the money entity, governmental entities, and memetic entities representing various philosophies and schools of thought. Rather than select a single corporation for our explorations, we will examine pertinent elements from a variety of corporations as we continue.

We will be discussing seemingly obvious aspects of these various entities. However, once again, Atem hopes that you will find revelation in how these aspects fit together and by understanding them in the frame of the presuppositions and behavior created by the mind of Atem.

ATTENTION

THE EXISTENCE OF A MEMETIC ENTITY depends on attention. Specifically directed attention is necessary for the entity's creation, and continued attention of various sorts is necessary for the entity to be maintained.

The initial creation process involves directing attention in such a way that you first define *what* you are giving attention to and then give it that specific attention. Again, we are forming the path by walking on it. We'll examine three ways in which this can happen.

Conscious Analysis

This is the most common method for creating memetic entities and also the one with the most varied results. Based on analysis of their situation, a human or group of humans decides that there is a need for a particular entity. An entrepreneur may see a warehouse full of products and decide that a corporation is necessary to market and sell those products. When communications researchers in the U.S.A. decided there was a need to share information between computers, they created ARPANET, the forerunner of the Internet. Eighteenth-century leaders who recognized opportunities for political change created structures for democratic governments.

For our purposes, conscious analysis can be simplified to say that if there is a need in your life or situation, you may consider whether or not a memetic entity would be an appropriate solution. Nonmemetic entities (simple evocations) and behaviors not directly related to entities are often appropriate solutions for most situations. The choice of a memetic entity may be dictated by the need for transmission, growth, autonomy, or interaction of large numbers of humans.

Unconscious Revelation

As you may have experienced while performing the Thirty-six Days of Atem exercises, outcomes can be suggested to parts of internal and external consciousness that are usually outside of awareness. The Making/Trance exercises, for instance, describe a straightforward method of developing a particular outcome and then receiving information about it through a process of ongoing revelation. Aikido was born of a similar process. Morihei Ueshiba practiced a variety of meditations and rituals, and the defining moment in which he realized that his martial skills could be realigned into a new, nonviolent art came with a spontaneous vision in which he saw Aikido. Unconscious revelation is also how Atem came into being.

The first and foremost advantage of unconscious revelation is that you may be inspired to create something that your conscious mind cannot predict. You may not consciously understand that there is a need for something, or there may not be a need for the entity, until you create that need along with the entity! Similarly, the nature of the entity may represent an unpredictable solution for a known problem.

Ask an Entity

This is probably the rarest method of all, and it may be considered a specific example of unconscious revelation. Very simply, it involves asking an existing entity for information about entity creation. For instance, you might evoke and ask the money entity for information about creating a corporation. Or you might ask Atem about the possibilities of entity creation. There are at least several religions that began in this way, with information gained from other entities. For instance, the Church of Latter Day Saints had its origin with information gained from a list of entities, including Jesus Christ, John the Baptist, and the prophet Elijah. The modern religion Thelema was based on information gained from an entity named Aiwass.

Of course, to continue to exist, a memetic entity requires continued attention from a larger number of humans. In some cases, the method for directing attention that was used to create an entity may also be the same as (or closely related to) the method used in conceiving the entity. For instance, in the case of Atem, some of the exercises given in this book are the same as those practiced to initially contact Atem. The actual birth process of Atem involved writing and publishing this book, while the transmission and continued existence relies in large part on humans reading the book. Attention directed in any way toward the book serves to feed Atem.

The money entity requires and receives a huge amount of attention. Indeed, many people spend the greater part of each and every day thinking about and working for the money entity. Every act related to employment presupposes the existence of the money entity. The money entity has proven that it can exist without paper or coin talismans, but those talismans continue to persist and are designed to support the entity in a variety of ways. Both coin and paper money are minted with symbolic representations, many of them relating to entities that support the money entity and serve to add power to it. Pictures of government leaders not only represent the government, but also very often are entities of myth and legend themselves. For instance, the myths and tales surrounding George Washington serve to remind us of the qualities of honesty, independence, and so forth in relation to the money. Every symbol, seal, letter, and number on paper money or coins is present to support the power and existence of the money entity.

Rock and roll's main source of attention is, of course, when people play or listen to rock music. Additionally, there are magazines, books, movies, and websites devoted to rock and roll. A host of lesser group minds and entities, ranging from bands at the smallest end to record companies at the larger, channel attention into the rock and roll entity.

Legba, like most other loas, takes his food directly. It is traditional to offer food—as well as cigars, candy, money, and alcohol—to loas. Food is a direct symbol of giving sustenance to the entity. Any offering that has meaning or value for the human who is offering will serve to direct attention and symbolic energy to the entity. Attention is also directed to Legba through the use of a Veve, a symbol that represents the loa; through the use of certain colors; and through drumming, using specific rhythms.

Attention is given to Aikido largely by practice. The more a human goes to a dojo and takes part in Aikido group practice, the more attention he or she is giving to the memetic entity. At the beginning of a practice session in most dojos, some attention is given to the memory of the founder, Ueshiba, in the form of bowing or by placing flowers or other offerings before a picture of him. In the same way that pictures of presidents lend attention to the money entity, so too do pictures of Ueshiba lend specific kinds of attention to Aikido. And, of course, Aikido practitioners offer attention even when not in the dojo, by reading books or magazines about Aikido, watching videos, visiting websites, thinking about Aikido, talking to other Aikidoists, and training on their own.

Democracy accepts its attention mostly in the form of votes, but also in the rhetoric of leaders, in political discussions and editorials, and so on. The rituals that surround the meetings of representative bodies, the images of great democratic leaders, and the symbolism of the various flags, seals, and emblems of the individual democracies all serve to direct attention to the entity.

The Internet accepts attention every time a modem connects, a web browser opens, a search engine is accessed, and with every single interaction that humans and other entities have with the vast network of computers and communication links.

Corporations accept attention in a variety of ways, including purchases of products or services, purchases of stock, and employment. Some, but not all, of this attention comes in the form of money. Some attention actually comes from the money entity. People working each day to meet the goals of the corporate entity may give greater or lesser amounts of attention. These people have agreed to devote attention to the entity for specific amounts of time each day. Corporate culture encourages specific behavior among employees, including dress, limits on recreational drug use, and interpersonal protocols. These limits not only serve to fit employees to the entity, but also act as offerings to the entity, comparable to giving a cigar to Legba. Corporations solicit attention through the use of marketing and advertising. Elements of marketing, including logo design, mottos and slogans, and advertising copy, serve to create a particular perception of the entity; these elements may or may not provide accurate representations of the entity, but nonetheless drive attention.

While the mechanisms in each of these entities may be different, the common factor is that each offers to fulfill a need for the humans who participate. The most successful entities offer something that addresses one or more of the basic drives of humans. Money offers survival and power. Rock and roll offers ecstasy, sex, power, and transcendence. Legba offers information and transcendence.

Aikido offers survival, health, resolution of conflict, and transcendence. Democracy offers power and security. The Internet offers mainly information, although that information may represent survival, power, sex, and transcendence. Corporations offer survival and power to their employees and a range of basic and not-so-basic needs to their customers, including sex, power, status, survival, health, and information.

The Basic Needs of Humans:

- **Survival.** Food, clothing, shelter, basic health.
- **Power.** Territory, possessions, influence over others.
- **Information.** Language, knowledge, science, problem-solving.
- **Sex and Status.** Ability to attract a mate.
- **Transcendence.** Altered states, "psychic" knowledge, ability to interact with entities, awareness of internal and external consciousness.

Atem offers mainly information and transcendence and, by opening the Way, may provide all other basic needs as well.

LANGUAGE

IN ORDER TO CREATE A MEMETIC ENTITY, you will need to have detailed and compelling descriptions. Ultimately, your outcomes will be projected in all senses, as they were in the Making/Trance exercises, and all of those senses can be described in written or spoken language. This description will assist you in numerous ways, serving as a reminder of important details, a method of exploring the power and practicality of your imaginings, and a record of the evolution of the entity, among other things. Elements of the description may prove directly useful in marketing and transmission. If your description includes the kind of language and submodality information that excites and inspires you, then rereading your written record will also serve to increase your own motivation.

Have patience and allow your description to build and feed back on itself as your understanding grows. Depending on the complexity of the memetic entity, new and more detailed information can be revealed throughout your days and nights as you begin to deepen contact with the entity. Write down information as it comes to you—memory is state dependent, and what you remember right after doing a particular exercise may be less accessible to you in other states of consciousness. Making notes while the information is fresh in your mind ensures that it will be available to you later.

Part of the description will be a list of qualities or elements that are essential to the entity. In the case of Atem, these are, of course, Attention, Language, Passion, Fitting, Trance, and Making. Every entity will have qualities that are necessary to it. You will understand what these are as your description grows and you start to notice what words are significant and repeated.

Possible elements of the money entity might include Value and Exchange along with the bits and pieces called dollars, pounds, yen, euros, and other units of exchange. The rock and roll entity certainly revolves around Rhythm, Melody,

Chord Structure, Release, Freedom, Expression, and so on. Elements related to Legba might be Ancestors, Crossroads, Opening, and Male. Aikido includes its elements in its name: in Japanese, *ai* means "harmony," *ki* means "life force," and *do* means "way." Elements for democracy might include People, Voting, Representation, and Freedom. The Internet might be understood in terms of Information, Users, Domains, Bandwidth, Email, Web, and so on. Corporations will each have their own list of elements, although some general ones might be Profits, Labor, and Management.

Along with a list of elements, you may also choose to create a list of powers. These powers are essential in terms of transmission. They tell the prospective participant what he or she will get in exchange for offering attention to the entity. Atem's powers, once again, are Communication, Neuroplasticity, Transformation, Transmission, Beauty, Understanding, Balance, and Opening. Money offers Power, Status, Equity, and Respect. Rock and roll offers Coolness, Mojo, Fun, Sex, and Drugs. Legba offers to Open the Gate. Aikido offers Health, Connection with the Universe, Self-defense, and Focus of Attention. Democracy offers Suffrage and Representation. The Internet offers Communication, Transmission, Knowledge, and Access. Corporations offer Wages, Products, and Services.

This list of elements and powers will become very important when you begin to address the aspect of passion. You may wish to revise or refine your list of elements at that time.

Another part of the description to be developed on the linguistic level will include the presuppositions that are inherent to the entity. How does the entity think? What kind of logical (or illogical) processes does it engage in? What basic statements about its reality can the entity make? The presuppositions, in effect, define the epistemology of the entity, the linguistic framework through which it perceives and defines both internal and external consciousness.

Atem has six basic presuppositions: everything is consciousness; the more flexible your behavior, the greater your ability to open the way; the more Atem is activated, the easier it is for everyone to open the way; the more often the way is opened, the more Atem is perpetuated; awareness can be located anywhere; a path is formed by walking on it.

Six is a favorite number of Atem; other entities may have more or fewer presuppositions. The behavior of some entities may hinge on a single presupposition. For instance, the Thelema religion/current/entity depends solely on an understanding of the phrase "Do what thou wilt shall be the whole of the Law." Other entities may have lengthy and complicated lists of presuppositions, conditions, and rules, as in the case of corporate by-laws. In general, entities that have fewer but broader presuppositions will tend to be more successful. "Broader" means that the concept will apply in more and more situations. For instance, "Employees must wear blue shirts on Tuesday" applies only in a very specific context. On the other hand, "For every action there is an equal and opposite reaction" can be extended to a very wide range of physical actions in the external consciousness and can also be applied as metaphor for human behavior, politics, and even spiritual processes.

Keep in mind that presuppositions are not necessarily "true." You might personally disagree with a presupposition that your memetic entity will hold dear. Presuppositions are a set of operating rules for the entity. Again, they are how the entity will think, for the purposes of achieving transmission and whatever specific purpose the entity may have been created to accomplish.

The money entity uses a few very broad presuppositions, including "Everything has its price," "You need money to live," "Time is money," and "Money is power." A complex system of rules and processes has grown up around these basic presuppositions, but these represent the core of the entity.

The presuppositions of the rock and roll entity may include "It's better to burn out than to fade away," "Sex is a positive quality," "Rock and roll can save your soul," "If it's too loud, you're too old," and "Stick it to the Man."

Legba's presuppositions might be phrased as "There is a human realm and a spirit realm," "The realms meet at the crossroads," "The other loas will come after you've summoned Legba," and "Make the right offerings and rituals and the spirits will appear."

Aikido's presuppositions may be found eloquently stated in the writings of Morihei Ueshiba, particularly in the volume *The Art of Peace*. These might be summed up as "Lead the mind and the body follows," "All techniques are transmitted person-to-person," "There is a way of harmony or resolution in all situations," "Everyone can find a level of training appropriate to them," "The place to start training is right where you are now," "Aikido is a celebration of human joined with heaven and earth," and so on.

The presuppositions of democracy might be found in statements and phrases such as "All men are created equal," "One person, one vote," "Checks and balances," and "Government is to serve the people."

The Internet entity will have a set of presuppositions that include, along with statements of a technical nature, statements that describe interaction, such as, "Every action that you make in cyberspace affects the Internet indefinitely"; "The memory of the Internet is held in your nervous system and body, in the nervous systems and bodies of all other elements of the collective, as well as in the digital memory of the computers"; "Deliberately changing your own consciousness and making consciously chosen actions in relation to the Internet can change the consciousness of the collective"; and "Acting in harmony or conformity with your own True Will will have the effect of harmonizing or purifying the general consciousness of the Internet."

Corporations, again, will each have a specific set of presuppositions that relate to specific elements of corporate structure and culture. General presuppositions used by many corporations may include "Everything affects the bottom line," "The customer is always right," and, in common with the money entity, "Time is money."

Your presuppositions can be created solely from the point of view of the entity. While your prospective participants may not yet think in these same terms, with the same presuppositions, your fitting techniques will bridge the gap. Very often, as in the case of Atem or Aikido, it is the purpose of the entity to teach this particular epistemology to the participants. In most other cases, it is not necessary for participants to consciously understand the presuppositions.

PASSION

ONCE YOU KNOW THE ELEMENTS AND PRESUPPOSITIONS of your entity, creating congruence is a fairly straightforward task. If you take everything you know about the entity and begin organizing it into categories reflecting the elements, you will immediately learn whether your plan has any deficiencies, any over-emphasized elements, and any superfluous material.

Remember that each category, for even greater congruence, can reflect the whole of the entity. Atem makes this explicit in, for instance, the Thirty-six Days of Atem, where each elemental section also addresses each of the other elements. The Attention exercises are divided up into Attention/Attention, Attention/Language, Attention/Passion, and so on for all of the elements. Then the language exercises follow as Language/Language, Language/Attention, Language/Passion, and so on. While this information is made obvious for Atem, it is mainly exhibited as a teaching tool; most memetic entities will not display this information, although the information will be available in some way to those who help the entity come into being and to the more dedicated participants.

Another level of congruence is attained when the participants and media artifacts used to transmit the entity exemplify the principles of the entity. For instance, the money entity is transmitted by money itself; rock and roll is transmitted by musicians who live the rock and roll lifestyle, who demonstrate their freedom and energy in sex, drugs, wild escapades, and with recordings and videos, the artwork of which also reflects the ideals of the entity. Legba is transmitted by the rituals, rhythms, and symbols unique to Legba and often by participants who have been possessed by the Legba spirit. Aikido is taught by those who have become proficient at Aikido and, at least while in the dojo, exemplify the principles of the art in every aspect of their being. Democracy is transmitted by political and economic policies of nations who have adopted a democratic system. The Internet exists through a system of fractally repeating networks of computers, fiber optics, local area networks, and so on, each portion of which resembles the greater network of the entire Internet. Corporations replicate offices, stores, outlets, and plants, each with an internal structure of workers that matches the overall corporate structure. This book, of course, demonstrates the elemental structure of Atem and is itself an example of how to create a memetic entity. In effect, Atem demonstrates by creating himself, by walking his own path, right now.

As demonstrated in the passion exercises of this book, increasing the energy and enthusiasm associated with the entity will also tend to increase congruence. The more that people want to have money—because of poverty, ambition, or avarice, for instance—the more attention they give to the money entity. From the very beginning, rock and roll has been known for audiences that screamed for their stars, tore up their seats, and danced into ecstasy. The bands most able to create these passionate responses have always been the most successful. Legba also offers powerfully ecstatic experiences of dance, rhythm, and possession. Aikido creates heightened states of awareness, experiences of time distortion, and a general increase in feelings of well-being; many Aikidoists describe their fascination and regular return to the dojo in terms of addiction, albeit a very positive one. Democracy, as with most governmental systems, uses rhetoric and mass experiences to motivate participants to vote, to serve in armed forces, and to support policies and actions of the elected representatives. Internet users also express their urge to participate in the Internet with metaphors of addiction; they are enjoying the mental stimulation, erotic stimulation, and mass experiences of the entity. Corporations use incentive programs, rhetoric, and salaries to motivate their employees.

Mass and group experiences, you may have noticed, are associated with all these memetic entities. It is in the nature of a memetic entity to encourage the participation of humans en masse. Humans minds are the major component of any memetic entity, and the more of them that are involved, the larger and more successful the entity. Being part of a group of any size offers humans the experience of acting with a greater magnitude and power than in their individual lives. Fully participating in a mass human experience is often akin to mystical experience. It gives direct experience of a greater whole, reflected in each of the parts.

The group mind is the basic form of a memetic entity, and participating in a true memetic entity offers experiences and sensations that can be obtained only in this way. These experiences may be exploited for great evil, as in the case of nationalism and fascism, or for great good, as in the U.S. peace and civil rights movements of the twentieth century or in the mass movements inspired by Mohandas Gandhi in India during that same time period.

This section has so far described the methods for exciting the participants, aiding in transmission, continuity, and congruence. Memetic entities themselves can also be roused and enthused. The energy of the participants feeds the enthusiasm of the entity, but these energies are not necessarily one and the same. The money entity gets excited or depressed as participants turn their attention toward local and world events of various kinds; wars and natural disasters may drive prices and sometimes profits up. The rock and roll entity has been excited about different rhythm variations, chord progressions, and musical subgenres over the years, including rockabilly, acid rock, punk rock, new wave, metal, grunge, and others. Note that with many of these styles, the entity became enthused, spread the new forms through the media, and then attracted swarms of participants. Legba is aroused by his rhythms, by dancing, by sex, by offerings of various types. He may appear to a participant, excited with unexpected and new information that he wishes the human to help transmit. Aikido is enthused by large-scale events, major conferences, and seminars. Democracy is excited by controversy and the competition of an election and also by the chance to throw off tyranny. The Internet is excited by any new trends that expand its powers, such as e-commerce and online pornography. Corporations are excited by publicity and profits.

FITTING

IN THE BEGINNING, IT IS IMPORTANT to fit the artifacts of an entity to your own strengths. For instance, if you are adept at creating video, but not at writing books, your first attempts to transmit your entity will likely be best served by video. If you are better at working up contracts and legal documents than you are at writing songs, then your entity may initially transmit best through contracts and documents. As a memetic entity spreads, other participants will carry the essence of the entity into other media. For instance, there are books and college courses about finance and money, books and documentaries about Aikido and rock and roll, tarot cards and scholarly dissertations about Legba and other loas, even though these are not the forms through which these entities originally came into being.

Your own creative strengths must be matched with the audience of prospective participants. In traditional marketing terms, you should recognize the demographics of your target audience. The initial media artifacts and transmission methods are best when fitted with the needs and desires of the potential participants. Is this audience a literate group who will purchase and read books? Do they prefer visual media such as video or film? Do they listen to the radio, or are they more apt to surf the Web? Will they prefer to attend a live event, concert, meeting, ritual, lecture, revival, or workshop, or will they prefer to hear about the entity from a friend, read about it in on a web page, or acquire it as a slogan from a t-shirt or bumper sticker?

The entry of a participant into the corpus of an entity may happen in stages, through a variety of media. A rock and roll fan may first hear a song on the radio, then attend a concert by the artist who created that song, then begin to purchase albums, concert tickets, and memorabilia from a wider range of similar musicians. A prospective Aikido practitioner might first be exposed to the form through word-of-mouth reports from friends, from public demonstrations, or from seeing a movie star use Aikido techniques in a film. This initial exposure might inspire him or her to begin attending classes and seminars. Humans may be drawn into the Internet by a particular activity—for instance shopping at an online auction site—then may begin to explore email, blogs, online news sources, and so on. Atem may make his first appearance to participants in these pages and inspire them to join a practice group; or, conversely, a prospective participant might attend a practice group, lecture, or seminar prior to reading the book.

In short, know your audience and start where you already have ability. As soon as your entity has been born, however, be prepared to expand your efforts or to have means in place to inspire other participants to carry the message further. Remember that an entity rarely exists in only one medium. The entity exists in the noosphere, and the media are expressions and tools of that consciousness. Just as a human may use spoken language, written language, sign language, music, mathematics, or a thousand other ways to communicate, so too may an entity communicate in diverse ways.

A new entity will offer to meet one or more of the basic human needs. While the bulk of the entity's media artifacts may not necessarily state this offer explicitly, it needs to be fairly near the surface of the content. Money always promises survival and power. Hit rock and roll songs are mainly concerned with sex ("I Want to Hold Your Hand," "Rock Me Baby," "Walk This Way"), power ("Pump It Up," "Games Without Frontiers," "Anarchy in the U.K."), and transcendence ("Break on Through," "Are You Experienced?" "Redemption Song"). Legba offers to guide participants through the crossroads to transcendence and power. Aikido offers survival in the form of self-defense and transcendence through practice of *ki* exercises. Democracy offers survival through the protection and services of a benevolent government. The Internet offers not only information, but also survival for those who earn their living online, power for those who succeed at earning their living online, sex and more sex, and the transcendent experience of being part of so vast an entity. Corporations offer survival for their employees and other specific basic needs for their customers, depending on the emphasis of the business.

Traditional marketing approaches will, more often than not, remain useful for distributing the media artifacts related to the entity. If you have a book, film, song, or product that aids in the transmission of the entity, you would do well to study effective marketing tactics, including press relations, advertising copy, and the business models associated with successful sales and distribution of similar books, films, songs, or products. Your entity will likely have additional input in this regard and may often be relied upon to help create powerful, specific, and unique marketing techniques.

TRANCE

TRANCE IS IMPORTANT THROUGHOUT THE EXISTENCE of a memetic entity. Indeed, it can be useful to define an entity as a particular trance or set of trances. For simplicity's sake, we'll address two primary areas of concern: the altered states necessary to create an entity and the altered states that attract and enable participants.

Altered States of Creation

Anything that enhances or inspires creativity in general is useful in the process of entity creation. Again, a memetic entity can be the essence of simplicity, conceived and manifested in a moment, or it can be a major work, consuming decades of time and involving hordes of humans. Even in the case of a simple evocation that proves to have the ability of memetic transmission, creating a memetic entity requires an act of genius, of revelation, to know exactly how this simple form will fit, transmit, and gather attention.

Consider the word *genius*. The ancient Romans used this word to refer to a guiding or teaching entity associated with a person or with a *gens*, meaning a clan or tribe. A technique for accessing wisdom or creativity, then, is to think with the mind of the genius entity. In this particular trance state, seemingly disparate ideas can be synthesized into new forms and systems, and processing and recall activities greater than that of an individual conscious mind can be performed.

Similarly, one may adopt trance states that are associated with any number of entities who may offer specific aid to the project at hand. For instance, it might help to think with the mind of the money entity when creating a new corporate structure, to think with the mind of the Internet when figuring out how to transmit an entity online, or to think with the mind of Atem when developing a new memetic entity. Legba and Aikido both participated in the creation of Atem in this way.

The specific techniques and exercises for achieving these trance states have already been outlined explicitly in earlier chapters of this book. Priming your creativity by accessing appropriate entities or by practicing the Making/Trance exercises can prove to powerfully assist a wide range of projects, not just the creation of memetic entities.

Continued use of these processes begins to develop altered states useful for accessing new ideas or syntheses and begins the process of developing the mind of the new entity itself. Every entity is associated with a particular trance that is defined through its epistemological presuppositions, the activities and media surrounding the entity, and experiences that the entity provides. As the feedback loop of creativity defines and develops the presuppositions, the media and the resulting experiences, the particular trance or trances that define the entity, will emerge.

Altered States of Participation

The activities and media that are offered to prospective participants must not only persuade or inform, but must also offer the opportunity to think with the mind of the entity, to have an experience beyond that of ordinary human consciousness. As well, they must promise results and spark the imagination of the prospective participant. It is in the imagination that the entity finds form.

Even the most cursory of participants with the money entity are immediately exposed to the presuppositions that define the entity's thoughts. You have to know that there is a price for something and that an exchange can be made. The promises of wealth and internal imaginings of oneself with the benefits of wealth—or the fear of imagined poverty—encourage participation.

The rock and roll entity invites participation in activities that are inherently trance inducing. The rhythms, instrumentation, dancing, and imagery of rock and roll all exemplify the presuppositions of the entity, more through example and practice than exposition. Rock and roll trances may be characterized by aerobic activity, rhythmic movement, and effects both physical and mental of exposure to high-decibel sound. The promises of ecstasy, salvation, and sex spark imaginings of enhanced self-worth.

Legba is traditionally contacted through religious ceremonies and ritual that, again, presuppose elements of the mind of Legba. Ritual elements such as rhythm, dancing, song, chanting, recitation, intoxication, and so on are, as with the rock and roll entity, inherently trance inducing. The trance state may include acts of devotion and sacrifice, a loosening of ego encouraged by music and dance, and full possession. In short, you approach Legba by deliberately engaging in his thought process. Legba promises to open the gates of the imagination itself.

Aikido's presuppositions are mostly hidden as metaphors within the form's movements. Application of Aikido principles in a wide range of situations often develops along with the physical skills. Each Aikido technique begins with an attack, utilizes the existing tendencies of the participants, and ends in resolution. These same principles spread as presuppositions, often without ever being explicitly stated. The movements themselves create an immediate altered state characterized by relaxed muscles and breathing, heightened but generalized external awareness, and time distortion. Over time, the trance offers access to the mind of the entity. The promises of peace and transcendence prompt the imagination toward conscious application of these principles in daily life.

Democracy's trance states are subtle but extremely pervasive. For someone living in a "democratic" nation, there is little choice but to participate at some level, even if only to grumble at the system, whether he or she personally agrees with democracy or not. The presuppositions are spread through ideology, through the point of view of media outlets within a democratic nation, and through education and indoctrination of the young. The trance state itself is associated with feelings of belonging and empowerment. Trance states of nationalism and patriotism often fuel and support the transmission of the entity, along with promises of security, prosperity, and protection from foes both real and imagined.

Accessing the Internet requires the participant to engage in very specific physical and mental activities. The participant must interface with a computer, turning attention toward the display or monitor; must think in terms of domain hierarchies and data transfer protocols; and use text, hypertext markup language (html), or streaming media within fairly narrow parameters. You can define this altered state within very close parameters in terms of posture, breathing, movement and so forth. Visual input is coordinated with hand movements on a keyboard, or other interface and linguistic skills are called into play. The state is replicable with a limited set of variations—and it evolves along with the hardware and content of the Internet. The Internet is created in large part by sheer imagination. It encourages and provides incentive for the development of imagination skills.

The caffeine- and alcohol-fueled mindset of the classic American corporation has evolved over the years, but the externally aware, fast-thinking altered state of the business world is still the trance of corporations. Cleverness, problem-solving activity, and concern about interpersonal behavior define the corporate mind. Promises of survival, wealth, and power encourage dreams of future corporate status.

Atem's trance states are initially the results of reading and practicing the exercises in this book, alone or with a practice group. After these states have coalesced into something closer to the mind of Atem itself, then the way is open to experience all trance states that are associated with entities of any type. The moment of having completed the creation of a new memetic entity is a very unique state in itself and one about which Atem hopes to spur the dreams of participants.

MAKING

1. Evoke Atem

ATEM, AS THE OPENER OF THE WAY, CAN ACT AS MEDIATOR between your conscious mind and all the parts of internal and external consciousness that may participate in the creation of a memetic entity. Atem can be contacted by the methods described in this book, particularly by practicing the Thirty-six Days of Atem exercises, on your own or with a practice group, and activating the book with a sigil. The activated book can then be used to quickly and easily contact Atem. Or, once contacted, Atem may suggest other quick and efficient methods to recontact him. An in-person initiation to Atem also adds power and efficiency to this process.

The evocation of Atem, projecting Atem into some area of external consciousness, may include or begin with invocation (bringing forth Atem into internal consciousness), but it is best when the operation ends with the externalized form. This externalized form of Atem is to be treated as you would a state entity in the Making/Trance exercise.

Interaction with Atem, as fully as possible, is more important than this set of instructions.

2. Develop an Outcome

Imagine the outcome of creating the memetic entity. Make it as complete as you can. Include all the senses, as much as possible. Create images, sounds, feelings, tastes, and smells of what your memetic entity will be like when it comes into existence. If you only have the barest idea or concept, use whatever small amount of information you have available and allow feedback from Atem over successive days and weeks to fill in the details until you are actually creating your entity.

In the beginning, place particular emphasis on the feelings that you will have upon completion of the project. What will it feel like to have brought into the world an entity with the capacity for transmission, an entity that has the potential for influencing or changing the lives of humans on a mass scale? What other senses can be used to create metaphors for this completion? Will the entity be shining? Singing? Glittering? Whirling? Humming? Use whatever submodalities have meaning to you and give you the appropriate feeling.

3. Offer the Outcome to the Universe

Give all of your perceptual creations relating to your outcome to Atem with instructions to pass it along to all the parts of internal and external consciousness that are necessary and appropriate for your outcome to be manifest. Do this at least daily, more often if possible, until your entity is completed.

4. Create Congruence in Your Life

Contrive the circumstances of your life to be in accordance with your entity. Make yourself a fitting creator for your entity. In most cases, doing this includes improving your health in whatever ways you can. Mental states are as important as physical health in this regard. Eat, sleep, work, and play in ways that create the appropriate mental states. Becoming an entity creator may also include removing distractions of various sorts from your life. And it will likely include placing within the range of your senses images, sounds, feelings, tastes, and smells that relate to the nature of your entity.

Live in accordance with your entity. Once it is born, you may be able to send it off and live in other ways, but during the birth process you will likely get the best results if you think with the mind of your entity as much as possible. Test your actions and beliefs with the presuppositions that you develop for your entity. Live as if these presuppositions were true. If you are creating a rock band as an entity, then dress and live as a rock star. If you are creating a corporation, then live as the executive that your entity would have you be. If you are creating a new school of philosophy, then live according to that philosophy.

5. Create Congruence in Your Entity

As you continue to offer your outcome to Atem and to develop more details about your entity, you can begin to fill in and organize the information according to a system of elements. Notice what categories your details naturally fall into. Think about what other categories might be necessary or particularly useful. Think about whether or not any of your existing details are not necessary or useful. Ask Atem about these issues and adjust the model of your entity accordingly.

Create a chart or outline based on your elemental system, filling in the various details. When you have a full and balanced set of elements, you are ready to bring the entity fully into manifestation.

6. Create the Media

Through what media will your entity manifest? Use the information that you are developing to create your books, images, videos, songs, architecture, by-laws, infrastructures, t-shirts, or whatever you will be using to transmit your entity. Make these media beautiful and appealing to prospective participants. Set your entity in motion to gather attention.

7. Unleash Your Entity

Continue to feed your entity attention and whatever else it needs to survive, but once it has been born, allow it to grow and act of its own accord. Be supportive, but get out of its way.

8. Observe and Record

Take some time to reflect on what you have experienced, to measure and observe the existence of your entity, and to make a record of the creation.

APPENDIX A:
RECOMMENDED STUDY

Andreas, Steve and Connierae Andreas. *Change Your Mind and Keep the Change*. Boulder, CO: Real People Press, 1987.

Bandler, Richard and John Grinder. *The Structure of Magic, Volumes 1 & 2*. Palo Alto, CA: Science and Behavior Books, 1975.

Bandler, Richard. *Using Your Brain for a Change*. Boulder, CO: Real People Press, 1985.

Behrend, Genvieve and Joe Vitale. *How to Attain Your Desires by Letting Your Subconscious Mind Work for You*. Garden City, NY: Morgan James Publishing, 2004.

Cunningham, D. M., et al. *Creating Magical Entities: A Complete Guide to Entity Creation*. Perrysburg, OH: Egregore Publishing, 2003.

Dilts, R. "Creating a 'We-Field': Evolving a Shared Resource (A 'We-Source') Through Somatic Syntax." NLP University, 1998, *http://nlpu.com/Patterns/patt21.htm*

DuQuette, Lon Milo. *My Life with the Spirits: The Adventures of a Modern Magician*. York Beach, ME: Weiser Books, 1999.

Erickson, Milton H. *Mind-Body Communication in Hypnosis*. New York: Irvington Publishers, 1986.

Farber, Philip H. *FutureRitual: Magick for the 21st Century*. Chicago: Eschaton Productions, 1995.

Hawkins, David. *Power vs. Force: The Hidden Determinants of Human Behavior*. Carlsbad, CA: Hay House, 2002.

Korzybski, Alfred. *Science and Sanity: An Introduction to Non-Aristotelian Systems and General Semantics*. 5th ed. Fort Worth, TX: Institute of General Semantics, 1995.

Kraig, Donald Michael. *Modern Magick*. Woodbury, MN: Llewellyn Publications, 2002.

La Tourrette, John. *Kahuna Secrets of How to Increase Your Vital Force*. Medford, OR: Sports Psychology Institute, 1999. Video.

Long, Max Freedom. *The Secret Science at Work*. Camarillo, CA: DeVorss & Company, 1953.

Mathers, S. L. MacGregor. *The Sacred Magic of Abramelin the Mage*. Mineola, NY: Dover Publications, 1974.

———. *The Goetia: The Lesser Key of Solomon the King*. York Beach, ME: Weiser Books, 1995.

Newcomb, Jason Augustus. *The New Hermetics.* Boston, MA: Weiser Books, 2004.

Reich, Wilhelm. *The Mass Psychology of Fascism.* 3rd ed. New York: Farrar, Straus and Giroux, 1980.

Shifflett, Carol M. *Ki in Aikido: A Sampler of Ki Exercises.* Berkeley, CA: North Atlantic Books, 1998.

Tohei, Koichi. *Ki in Daily Life.* Tokyo: Japan Publications Trading Company, 2001

Ueshiba, Morihei. *The Art of Peace.* Boston, MA: Shambhala, 2002.

Vitale, Joe. *Spiritual Marketing: A Proven 5-Step Formula for Easily Creating Wealth from the Inside Out.* Bloomington, IN: Authorhouse, 2001.

Wilson, Robert Anton. *Prometheus Rising.* Tempe, AZ: New Falcon Publications, 1992.

APPENDIX B:
LIST OF SUBMODALITIES

Visual

Number of images

Size of image

Self in picture or out of picture
 (perceptual positions)

Movement/stillness

Brightness

Contrast

Color/black and white

Shade/hue

Location of image in aura

Center weighted/wide angle

Focus

Light source

Background

Duration

Frame or border

Depth

Two- or three-dimensional

Shape of image

Auditory

Number of sounds/sources

Volume

Tone or voice

Rhythm

Cadence

Range

Pitch

Resonance

Intonation

Inflection

Duration

Location of source

Harmony

Stereo/mono/balance

Background sounds

Kinesthetic

TACTILE

Type of feeling (tingling, pressure, temperature, weight, lightness, etc.)

Duration

Texture

Movement

Location

Speed

VISCERAL OR EMOTIONAL

Movement

Location in body

Duration

Type of feeling

Olfactory and Gustatory

Pungent

Aromatic

Sweet

Sour

Salty

Bitter

Earthy

Spicy

APPENDIX C
LIST OF VERB PREDICATES AND OTHER SENSORY WORDS

Visual

See	Crystal clear	Sparkling
Watch	Peruse	Shimmering
Reflect	Darken	Scene
Glow	Elucidate	Image
Eclipse	Vision	Imagine
Disillusion	Envision	Twinkle
Blank	Examine	Glance
Enlighten	Observe	Vague
Gaze	Illustrate	Obscure
Oversee	Outlook	Picture
Overshadow	Horizon	Paint
Illuminate	Color	Foresight
Peer	Scan	Frame
Clear	Flash	Transparent
Foggy	Brilliant	
Focused	Blazing	

Auditory

Say	Rumor	Din
Talk	Loud	Cacophony
Hear	Silence	Resonate
Rhythm	Oral	Mention
Beat	Gossip	Growl
Remark	Hum	Retort
Swear	Purr	Wail
Pronounce	Deaf	Overtone
Roar	Mellifluous	Question

Attune
Harmony
Squeak
Groan
Announce
Voice
Argue
Tune

Sing
Chime in
Whine
Shrill
Boisterous
Articulate
Click
Dissonance

Raspy
Tell
Mute
Audible
Snap
Buzz
Crunch
Cry

Kinesthetic

Touch
Grope
Throbbing
Crush
Backbone
Run
Walk
Rough
Smooth
Vibrate
Roll
Rock
Catch
Tension
Stress
Equilibrium
Cold
Hot
Feel

Relax
Visceral
Firm
Pull
Push
Break
Feverish
Tight
Rigid
Passive
Active
Tranquil
Emotional
Joyful
Lonely
Exuberant
Aroused
Horrified
Perturbed

Suffer
Terrorized
Warm
Annoy
Crushed
Happy
Sad
Depressed
Mad
Glad
Tired
Pressured
Blissful
Frustrated
Upset
In touch with
Calm
Passionate

Olfactory/Gustatory

Stink	Sweet	Musty
Smell	Sour	Putrid
Flowery	Peppery	Rancid
Nibble	Fishy	Fetid
Savor	Rotten	Bland
Taste	Disgusting	Aromatic
Digest	Smoky	Fragrant
Palatable	Pungent	Tasty

Unspecified

Ponder	Perceive	Believe
Congruent	Understand	Sense
Calibrate	Think	Conceive
Discern	Learn	Realize
Experience	Process	Comprehend
Ambiguous	Decide	Emphasize
Sensitive		

GLOSSARY

Epistemology: The study of the presuppositions behind knowledge and beliefs; a basic approach toward creating one's own reality.

Evocation: The act of moving something—an idea, a state, a feeling, an image, a sound, a quality, a memory, a work of art, or an entity from internal consciousness to external consciousness.

External consciousness: Those thoughts and experiences that we generally hold as being outside our minds or bodies.

Internal consciousness: Those thoughts and experiences that we generally hold as being inside our minds.

Invocation: The act of bringing something—an idea, a state, a feeling, an image, a sound, a quality, a memory, a work of art, or an entity—from external consciousness to internal consciousness.

Memetics: A meme is to information what a gene is to life. A meme is a unit of information that has the ability to spread from human to human. Memetics is the study of how memes are spread through the realm of consciousness, just as genetics is the study of how traits are passed through the realm of a species.

Memetic entity: A consciousness based in memes, just as human consciousness is based in genes.

Neurolinguistics/neurolinguistic programming (NLP): The study of the structure of subjective experience, a field of practice developed by Richard Bandler and John Grinder, influenced by the work of Alfred Korzybski, Gregory Bateson, Noam Chomsky, Milton Erickson, and others.

Noosphere: The realm of consciousness of all humans, composed of our thoughts, our communication, and media of every type.

Submodalities: The modalities referred to are the senses: visual, auditory, kinesthetic, olfactory, and gustatory. Submodalities are the distinctions that can be made within each sense, including whether or not some perception is internal, external, large, small, close, distant, and so on. See the "List of Submodalities" in appendix B.

Unconscious mind: Whatever is in your awareness now is conscious, your conscious mind. Everything else is your unconscious mind.

ABOUT THE AUTHOR

PHILIP H. FARBER is the author of *FutureRitual: Magick for the 21st Century* and has produced several DVD packages on magical topics, including *Magick for the 21st Century, Essential Meta-Magick,* and *Meta-Magick Invocation.* He is an instructor for Maybe Logic Academy, a certified hypnotist and a licensed trainer of neurolinguistic programming, and has a private practice in New York's Hudson Valley. Visit him at *www.meta-magick.com.*

TO OUR READERS

WEISER BOOKS, AN IMPRINT OF RED WHEEL/WEISER, publishes books across the entire spectrum of occult and esoteric subjects. Our mission is to publish quality books that will make a difference in people's lives without advocating any one particular path or field of study. We value the integrity, originality, and depth of knowledge of our authors.

Our readers are our most important resource, and we appreciate your input, suggestions, and ideas about what you would like to see published. Please feel free to contact us, to request our latest book catalog, or to be added to our mailing list.

Red Wheel/Weiser, LLC
500 Third Street, Suite 230
San Francisco, CA 94107
www.redwheelweiser.com